I've Never Made Anyone Rich

...(and why you still need a Financial Advisor)
2nd Edition

By M. Scott Brown with Laura Schaefer

I've Never Made Anyone Rich

Copyright © 2024 M. Scott Brown

All rights reserved. This book may not be photocopied for personal or professional use. No part of this book may be reproduced, stored in a retrieval system, or transmitted in any form or by any means (electronic, mechanical, photocopying, recording, or otherwise) without permission in writing from the author or publisher.

Second Edition

Produced in the United States

I've Never Made Anyone Rich

This book is dedicated to hardworking financial advisors everywhere. I hope it makes your lives a little easier. ~MSB

I've Never Made Anyone Rich

2024 Preface (Introduction: The Sequel)

Back in 2019, I wrote the book you are now holding. To say it wasn't a worldwide success is being kind. The truth is I never intended to sell a lot of books or in any way make my living as an author (thankfully). My intention was to put on paper my many experiences over a then 32-year and now 37-year career as a Financial Advisor. Hopefully, the few folks who did take the time to read it realized that investing – and more importantly, accumulating wealth sufficient to maintain them and possibly future generations – is not as complex as many would have us believe.

The introduction I wrote in 2019 is still in this updated version and remains relevant, whilst many of the facts and figures I included then needed updating. One example would be Bitcoin. As I type, it is set to open at around $67,000.00 dollars...up dramatically from the $12,000.00 it was in 2019 when I mentioned it in my introduction. It would be fair for you to now point out that had you bought Bitcoin at the 2019 price, you would have had a fantastic return. You may also point out that I suggested Bitcoin could not save you from poor investing habits.

My response would be (and is) that I was not wrong to suggest Bitcoin wouldn't save you from bad investing habits and poor emotion-based decision-making. Yes, Bitcoin did rise from about 12k to 67k (and fluctuated wildly over that time as well), a dramatic increase in value over a relatively short interval. But the fact remains that you likely did *not* buy at $12,000.00...and, more importantly, now feel tempted to chase it at $67,000.00. So, had you bought Bitcoin at $12,000.00, you would have been more lucky than good.

I'm not disputing the merits or lack thereof of Bitcoin as a good long-term holding – although I have some rather strong feelings on the matter. I am, however, saying that a long-term "wealth accumulation" plan that stands a high probability of being successful is not a series of brilliantly timed decisions. It is a long and tedious process that involves more effort than genius. Wealth accumulation is not complex, but it is hard.

It's hard because it requires ignoring the noise about Bitcoin, Top Secret Real Estate Deals, and Private Equity that can't miss (but often does). To be clear, I have missed out on many, check that, *almost all* the high profile get-rich-quick opportunities that have come across my purview over my now 37-year career. Microsoft IPO...nope, Apple IPO...nope, Bitcoin at $50.00...nope, Real Estate in 2005...nope. And today's darling, AI-based stocks like Nvidia...NOPE!

At this point, you might be wondering why I am starting a book on wealth accumulation and maintenance with a substantial, albeit incomplete, list of what you might call "mistakes" I have made.

The reason is simple: I do not see them as mistakes. I see them as random events I could not have predicted, nor do I care that I didn't.
You see, I am by all measures "wealthy." My net worth puts me in the top 2% of all Americans. Now, to be clear, I am not a billionaire, nor could I afford a private jet anytime soon. Many are substantially wealthier than I am. Not the point. The point is that a knucklehead kid from rural Florida (with grades just good enough to allow his high school teachers to rationalize graduating him) has succeeded to a degree because I understand that "getting lucky" is based on possibility, not probability.

The probability of participating in a Bitcoin surge or buying a piece of real estate one day and having someone offer you twice that amount the next is ridiculously low, somewhere just north of winning the lottery or finding a rare coin in your yard. Yes, these things happen, but likely not to you. In fact, it's the rarity of these "luck"-based outcomes that make them newsworthy. If everyone bought Bitcoin at $50.00 and quadrupled their money, then no one else would care.

The pages that follow are all about "probability" not "possibility." They're about the most likely path to wealth and a financially stable life. You don't need to invent a widget or run a tech company to be comfortable. What you need is emotional discipline. Statistically, way more people have lost money on Bitcoin than have made it.

"How can this be, given its meteoric rise?" you might ask.

Because most people, as Charlie Munger once said, "operate out of envy even more so than greed."

Envy makes you buy Bitcoin at $60,000.00 because you feel left out. Envy makes you buy a car you can't afford because your friend has one. Envy makes you spend more at dinner because you think it will impress those around you.

In the end, like 2019, it's not *complex*, it's just *hard* to accumulate wealth. Investment firms and trading platforms want you to believe they have the secrets and if you use their products or their programs with lots of blinking lights and fancy research, you won't have to do the hard part because they have done it for you. I think you know better than this. Or do you?

In the pages ahead, I outline the many emotional things folks do to sabotage their success and I provide a clear path for doing the hard things that are required to reach your financial goals. Millions of Americans are now millionaires not because of a shortcut or a lucky lottery ticket. Millions of regular folks are now millionaires because they understand that the probability of success is much higher by implementing a long-term disciplined approach to their wealth accumulation. To be fair, a few people get rich using shortcuts.

To quote the great Scott Galloway, "Assume you won't be one of them."

Peace,

Scott

Introduction

If you've ever stood next to a doctor at a party, you know sooner or later that poor physician—who just wants to enjoy her Old Fashioned and chicken skewer in peace—is going to be asked about someone's chronic back pain or odd skin rash. It's the same situation if you stand next to a financial advisor at a party, only the questions *we* get asked make a lot less sense. Thirty years of trying to keep a straight face near the chip dip as someone discusses flipping houses with his whole IRA is going to give me a stroke. Good thing there's a doctor nearby.

I can't take it anymore, so three decades of being a semi-friendly, mostly polite neighborhood financial advisor ends here. In his place is a "no bullshit, just the facts ma'am" guy who will no longer tolerate all the self-righteous, over-opinionated and under-informed nonsense I've been fielding for years.

No, I won't buy you Bitcoin; no, squirreling away gold bars won't save you from the apocalypse; no, you shouldn't buy every stock that ends in .com; and no, the Nigerian Prince will not be depositing $10 million in your checking account just as soon as you pay the "Nigerian Wealth Tax." NO! NO! NO! and hell no!

Over the last decade or so, I have written a column that is two parts education for the masses and one part therapy for an often-frustrated financial advisor. Without a doubt, my favorite thing to write about is behavioral economics, behavioral finance—the way people behave and how contrary it is to their own interests, despite me telling anyone who will listen, repeatedly, that the harebrained scheme they're explaining is not a great idea, that it is not going to work out the way they think it will: "I've seen people do all kinds of ridiculous, stupid, harmful things to their finances. What you're doing is likely one of them."

Often, my new party friend is doing one of the many things I warn against, but they will take another person's word over mine because people love it when someone agrees with them.

In the pages that follow, I hope to expand on each of the many conversations I've had and columns I've written—minus the touchy-feely filter—in an effort to get to the point and erase any doubt about the barrage of industry and media bull you have to wade through to make thoughtful decisions about your finances.

Why am I doing this and why should you care?

For starters, American capitalism has become a winner-take-all proposition, and every financial advisor you meet is probably selling you something. Again, in some way, everyone IS SELLING YOU SOMETHING. This, in and of itself, is not a bad thing. We all sell in some way, shape, or form, but my industry is so full of crap that the people selling it sometimes don't even know that they themselves are also victims of the system.

As a result, Average Joe or Jane Investor is often facing an aggressive market of people offering advice (sometimes bad).

The good news is that I'm probably never going to meet you. Therefore, I have no way to make money off you unless you bought this book and intend on buying ten more for friends and family (by all means, do that). In short, I have no reason to bullshit you. Think of me as a disinterested guide taking you behind the scenes of financial planning to cut through the jargon and discuss the tragic mistakes so many people can make when it comes to money. With this book, you can get educated and make smarter decisions.

After reading, the topics you should expect to have a better grasp on include:

- The extent to which the media is full of crap, and why you shouldn't put too much stock in what a 26-year-old "reporter" thinks.
- Why some advisors are worthless, and why those who aren't are worth more than you could ever pay them.
- Why Wall Street doesn't care *what* you buy, just *that* you buy.
- Why you're so sure there is a secret, even though there are no secrets to investing.
- The reason that obsessing over fees is largely a waste of time once you know exactly what you're paying for.
- How to find a great financial advisor—and reduce your layers of costs at the same time.
- Why the richest people I know rarely even think about their investments.

My goal has been, and will always be, to shed light on the things you can do as an investor to better your situation—and help you reflect on those things you can control versus those you cannot.

John Quincy Adams once said, "My aim is to protect your interests against your inclinations."

My aim is much the same. I'm just not much of a diplomat.

I've Never Made Anyone Rich

TABLE OF CONTENTS

Section One: Emotions & Behaviors

Chapter 1	The truth about money	15
Chapter 2	I don't make anyone rich	33
Chapter 3	Things the ideal client does	57
Chapter 4	What the misguided client focuses on	69
Chapter 5	How to stay calm in the chaos	83
Chapter 6	The media and the "experts"	101
Chapter 7	Reflections on 37 years in the business	113
Chapter 8	What comes after success	137

Section Two: Products & Practical Tips

Chapter 9	How to work with your advisor	151
Chapter 10	Products and buzzwords	187
Chapter 11	Risk	217

Section Three: For My Advisor Friends

Chapter 12	Think long-term	231
Conclusion	Same as it ever was	237

Reflection	245
Acknowledgments	247

Section One

Emotions & Behaviors

Chapter 1
The Truth about Money

On your deathbed, you will receive total consciousness. So I got that goin' for me, which is nice. ~Carl Spackler

What is wealth?

How do I know that the "money," or, more correctly, the data or digits on my electronic bank statement, are really there? I mean, can I touch it? Can I go visit it on the weekend, kinda like a relative in jail? How do I know that when I write a check and invest my life savings, it's not going straight to an account in the Cayman Islands? How do I know when I send a check to a charity that some round fella in a white suit and a cowboy hat (think Boss Hog) isn't spending my money on cigars and imported BBQ sauce?

How indeed.

Life is just one big roll of the dice. The foundation of our economy and our financial system is 100% based on risk and trust. Our forefathers and mothers set out across the vast wilderness that is now interstates and Waffle Houses not really knowing what they would find. Sure, they knew a little and they "trusted" that what they didn't know, they could overcome.

Sometimes they were right; more often, they were buried along the way.

They *didn't* know. They didn't know what they would find, and they didn't know if they would even live to try to find whatever "it" was.

"Knowing," in my mind, is overrated. Classically defined, a "risk offset" is the difference between the risk you take and the skill you have. In short, me trying to box Mike Tyson is a huge and likely pointless risk to take when one considers my skill level. Conversely, me trying to make a nice veggie lasagna from a recipe is indeed a risk, but a smaller one. The risk is simply that I may end up at a pub for dinner (which, honestly, seems like a reward to me) if I don't successfully combine the ingredients.

Knowing is no fun and almost never profitable. We *know* that if we go to the bank and buy a Certificate of Deposit we will earn a really crummy rate of return. We *know* if we never leave the house, it is unlikely that we will be run over by a bus or eaten by a tiger. We *know* that if we don't befriend someone, they can never disappoint us or do us harm. These are things we know.

For my money and yours, knowing is a waste of time and generally unprofitable.

Now, for those of you who enjoy exaggeration, I am not saying you shouldn't investigate and measure the risk you are taking compared to what you know about the endeavor. Whether we are talking investments (and we *are* talking investments in this book, right?), travel or relationships, there is a level of risk offset that we can do. Knowing a little more than the next guy is highly profitable. Learn as much as you can about the investment, travel destination, or individual. Then, at some point, you have no choice but to make a decision. Usually, the decision boils down to one thing: trust. Do I trust the romantic interest, the travel agent, or the financial person? Do I trust my instincts, my education, or my intuition?

The biggest mistake folks often make is not born of bad decisions.

It is almost always the result of no decision.
Money is Taboo and People are Intimidated

It's a huge problem; we don't even talk about it in school. I don't think you need to talk about money in the sense of, *I make this much,* or what you have or don't have. But knowing basics like *how does compound interest work?* Or, *how does the stock market work? Why is the Dow 25,000 and it used to be 2,000?*

Ninety-nine percent of the population doesn't even know why that happens. Nearly half of the country has nothing—zero dollars—invested in the market. These individuals have no money in pension funds, 401(k) retirement plans, IRAs, mutual funds or index funds, and it's not just due to a lack of money.[1] One Bankrate survey revealed 25% of people avoid the market because they don't understand stocks, 11 percent say stocks are too risky, and 7 percent say they don't trust stock brokers or financial advisors.[2]

The conversation needs to start in public schools. Since I first published this book, several school systems have begun to add Financial Basics to their curricula, which is clearly a step in the right direction. Several states have developed or are developing a curriculum for their high school students, including my home state of Florida. Additionally, the Dow industrial average now sits at 39,000, an increase since I first wrote these words of about 56%. Simply put, if you had done nothing else after reading this

---

[1] According to the Federal Reserve and numerous surveys by Gallup and Bankrate.
http://www.chicagotribune.com/business/ct-americans-dow-22000-investing-20170803-story.html
Accessed December 26, 2017.
[2] http://www.businessinsider.com/why-so-few-millennials-invest-in-the-stock-market-2016-7
Accessed December 26, 2017.

section but buy an ETF in the Index, you'd be looking at a $500.00 gain on every $1,000.00 you invested. It's not sexy but it *is* damn effective. Still, our education system largely teaches people to be employees and consumers. For the people who sell stuff and need employees—which is most corporations—it's a wonderful feeding system.

Despite this somewhat depressing situation, resources are available for those who want to learn. They're just not in an easy-to-swallow pill form. It takes effort, like anything else. If we build those muscles early in school, in elementary school, in middle school, and in high school especially, that curiosity will carry over. Young people will have a foundation to build on.

The reason we don't have the discussion—about money—is people are *embarrassed* by the discussion. They don't know what to ask, which is also the reason people walk into a financial advisor's office and agree with whatever that advisor says. They're embarrassed to ask a question that might come across as stupid. Their reticence is making them vulnerable because they are *not* asking the questions. The fear is what's blowing them up. If we're not all talking about what Wells Fargo did to piss everybody off—because we don't *quite* understand it—then Wells Fargo, in this example, has no reason to behave differently. They know most people don't have the intellectual resources to understand what they (Wells Fargo) just did, so they simply pay the fine and get back to business as usual.

We have *made* money talk taboo. We have intentionally coded the industry and the business with jargon that nobody understands, and that, frankly, doesn't mean anything. The more jargon a person uses, the less likely it is they know what they're talking about. They want to confuse you so you don't ask questions.

The Dumb Stuff People Believe about Money

People believe they can save their way to wealth, and I don't mean save money. They believe they can negotiate or discount transactions to wealth. Meaning, if I spend six months shopping for a car rather than spending six months working a second job, I'll get rich. People have been conditioned to believe the former rather than the latter is the way to go. When, in fact, it's not even close.

Making money in the margins is how people get rich. They don't work a nine to five and get their three percent raise each year, and cut coupons to wealth. They work their nine to five, put their butts in an Uber and work at night, save that money, and start their business. *That's* how many people get wealthy.

The media has convinced people they should research their way to wealth, so they're saying to themselves, "If I just find the right stock or the right formula, or the right mutual fund and insurance product, that will solve all my problems." Lean in for a second...NO!

NOPE. And it just never ends.

People believe money is finite. They believe that if another person has a lot, they themselves can't have more because the other person already has it.

This mentality can best be described as a "scarcity" mindset. Scarcity-minded folks are always counting the French fries on their neighbor's plate or wondering if they got the smallest piece of chocolate cake (okay, that is fair). Conversely, "abundance" minded folks see no end to the possibilities. Maybe you got more fries today but I'll likely be able to order more next time. The fact that you are successful has no bearing on *my* outcomes.

Many folks see financial transactions as finite: "If I don't get in on this deal I'm screwed and doomed to lifelong failure." Investing, however, is not a finite journey with a beginning and an end. Investing is an infinite engagement with all kinds of potential good and bad outcomes. When you see it as finite, you tend to overreact in the short term, pinning the success of an 80-year journey on the outcome of a single investment on any given day.

Investing, my impatient friends, is an all day, every day, you-open-your-eyes kind of thing. Processes built out of straw or involving short-term outsized outcomes (see crypto, .com stocks, and house flipping in '08) are more than likely going to result in your house being blown down. Conversely, processes built of long-term discipline and only dependent on reasonable long-term returns will resist even the most determined of Big Bad Wolves.

More frequently than I'd like, I will have a client who, at least for the moment, gets caught up in the short-term scarcity mindset: "Scott, you need to get me out of this market before it all goes to heck in a handbasket."

"So, what you're saying, Mr. Client, is that if I do not put all of your money in cash right now, the next 25 years of your life are likely ruined?"

You, who has been with me for 20 years and weathered four serious downturns and still managed to earn 6-8% annually? You, who spent nearly 5% annually of your nest egg since you retired five years ago and currently have more than you started the journey with? Furthermore, Mr. Impulsive, are you telling me large corporations like John Deere, ATT, Microsoft, Coke, Salesforce, Nike, Apple, Proctor & Gamble, and Kraft are all going out of business, but somehow the cash, and more importantly the institution you have your cash in, will be totally fine when the dust settles and the zombies relent? Mr. Impulsive, I think you see you're being quite silly here...don't you?

Scarcity-minded folks believe that when they enter a transaction with somebody, especially in this day and age (the mindset I'm talking about seems to be getting worse and worse), they have to get the better of that person. If they don't win and win big, they haven't won at all.

As recently as 30 years ago when I started in the business, two people could sit across from one another at a table, and when a transaction was about to occur, the feeling would be *I want to win and I want you to win. Because I know if you don't win, it's not a good transaction for either one of us. You'll be angry, and there are repercussions to that.*

People don't think this way anymore. Scarcity affects us in many ways. It affects – in my not-so-humble opinion – the way we treat each other. In days gone by, folks could sit down and hammer out a deal each party thought was fair. Each party would leave the table feeling they had gained some value by having interacted with the other. In the days of my youth (cue Led Zeppelin) my grandfather had a decent-sized citrus farm in rural Pasco County Florida. He would often trade bushels of oranges for a variety of things he might need from someone else. Maybe ii was fertilizer or possibly another crop for his and my grandmother's personal consumption.

Regardless of what the transaction consisted of, I never felt like either man (it was usually a man in those days) intended on beating the other out of anything above a fair trade. They both understood at some level that they needed each other and being less than fair in any given transaction would result in bad feelings and, more importantly, put an end to the symbiotic relationship they had formed.

This may be the old man in me, but I dare say the vibe has changed. Today, many folks have no qualms with extracting value from a relationship with no intent of returning it. The guy who spends three hours in the Local Appliance Store asking a million questions at the expense of the salesperson's time only to go home and buy it online for twenty bucks less is but one example of this new and in my opinion, less thoughtful way of doing business.

The Randomness of Life, Weather, and Money

For the most part, my clients have been trained and see a lot of these issues the same way that I do. The national dialogue is what irritates me—the everyday conversations I have to endure when somebody finds out I'm a financial advisor.

I don't even *like* money that much. I really don't. Ironically, I think I went into the right occupation given this stance, because I'm not *enamored* with money. Love of money doesn't cloud my conversations or my decisions. I grew up very lower middle class-ish, on a good day, and I always thought I wanted to be rich, whatever that meant—frankly, I didn't know what that meant. I wanted *things.* Yet when I acquired some comfort, and some *things,* for a little while that was satisfying, but largely over time, it wasn't. I see how people obsess about their money, and it's pointless. It's like obsessing about the weather. *I hope it doesn't rain!* They're wringing their hands. *And if it rains, it's going to be terrible! If it's a sunny day, I want to go outside, but how do I know it's not going to rain?*

On, and on, and on...

Accepting the randomness of life is so important, and that applies to money just as much as everything else.

John D. Rockefeller said, "We pursue perfection, but there is no absolute perfection in life, only near perfection. If you wait until all conditions are perfect, you can only wait forever, and the opportunity will be given to others."

Or, as Zach Brown more recently and succinctly put it in reference to making your mark in life, "When the pony he comes riding by, you better set your sweet ass on it."

The Value of Your Time: Is a Penny Saved a Penny Earned? Not Really

Let's address the 30-40% of you who are saying, "Financial advisor? I don't need no stinkin' financial advisor."

I get it.

I would actually say there *is* a group of folks who do not need and should never hire an advisor. Those people have both the ability and desire to keep track of their investments, dividends, income, tax reporting, legislative changes, beneficiaries, Required Minimum Distributions, contribution limits, stock research, bond inventories, Monte Carlo simulations, capital gains, proxy voting, inflation issues, Social Security calculations, trust funding, and, of course, Jim Cramer's outfit of the day.

There is just a hint of sarcasm in the preceding list, but I do sincerely concur that there are some folks who could and should do these things for themselves. I assure you, however, that the list of those folks is a lot shorter than the trading platforms advertised on TV would have you believe. In fact, I am constantly surprised at the folks who tell me they are going it alone. They are almost never individuals of means.

According to a study published by Northwestern Mutual in 2023, 70% of all millionaires work with a Financial Advisor versus 37% of the general population. Oftentimes when I quote a number like this some folks will be cynical.

I hear things like, "Well yeah, they can afford it," or, "No way am I spending money on something like that."

There are a lot of things wrong with these statements, but let's cut to the most obvious one. What you are saying – or thinking but not saying – is: "I would like to be a millionaire but I will not do what millionaires disproportionality do in order to attain and maintain their current economic status."

It's like saying, "Everyone I know who is in good shape eats little to no sugar, but I'm going to eat Oreos for dinner every night to achieve a slim and healthy body."

Now, to be fair, I realize I'm talking my book here (both literally and figuratively), but the facts are, well, the facts. Wealthy people prefer the second set of eyes and ears. The benefits and cost analysis are a bit nuanced to get into here in this general discussion but trust me, they exist, and I'll address some of them later in the book.

The reason wealthy people seek advisory relationships is not because they are, in fact, wealthy. Rather, it is because they value their time at a higher rate than those who choose to go it alone. What it all boils down to, simply, is time. What is yours worth?

If you have never read the book *The E-Myth,* I highly recommend it. *The E-Myth,* written by Michael Gerber back in 1988, changed my life and ultimately the way I approach business.

Most people spend an inordinate amount of time trying to save money, not realizing the actual cost of underutilizing that time. HUH? I will cite a good friend of mine as an example. My friend takes great pride in his car shopping skillz (spelled with a Z to show how cool he was in the 90s). He would spend literally a month going from dealership to dealership working his deal. Each week, I would estimate this guy spent nine or 10 hours traveling throughout his area "working over" the salesmen, pitting one against the other. Finally, after a month or so of plying his trade, he ended up working the deal of a lifetime and saving around $2,000 on his purchase.

At this point, you may be siding with our hero, "the slayer of car salesman." Not so fast, Huckleberry. A quick computation of our hero's time tells us he spent around 44 or so hours negotiating this deal. This, of course, does not account for time at home on the internet, nor the fifteen editions of *Consumers Digest* he read each night. In short, our friend has around 50 hours into this quest, which on the surface seems worth it. Or does it?

According to data from the Bureau of Labor Statistics, the median earnings for Americans aged 45-54 is roughly $64,428 per year.[3] If you divide that figure by the approximately 2,000 working hours in a year, you get about a $32 dollar per hour cost of your time. Doing some quick math, this means our hero lost around

---

[3] https://www.forbes.com/advisor/business/average-salary-by-age/ Accessed February 15, 2024.

$1,600.00 in time for a net savings of $400.00. Still not bad, you say?

Well, my friend would assert that not only did he net $400.00, but actually, he did this in his "free" time and therefore, it is still a net $2,000.00. Poppycock!

I don't know about you, but I value my free time at nearly twice the rate of my work time. In other words, time spent with my family and children is worth considerably more to me than time at work...AND I LOVE MY WORK!

Using this measure, our hero has spent nearly $3,200.00 of his time to find a net loss of $1,200.00. This story is not to diminish the savings of $400.00, $2,000.00, or any savings for that matter. *It is to make you stop and think before you bend over to pick up a penny while dollars fly over your head.*

The guy in my example makes considerably more than the average American, which actually causes him to suffer an even bigger loss when accounting for his time. Had he just haggled for a half hour at the first dealership, bought the car and gone back to work, he would have been considerably ahead. I realized long ago that changing my own oil, doing my own taxes, and giving up time with my kids was not an efficient use of my time or money.

Of course, you need to do these calculations for yourself and decide what makes mathematical sense. Your mileage may vary.

Scarcity vs. Abundance: It's All in Your Head

My uncle believes everything should be cheap, as cheap as possible. He wants certainty in his life. My uncle, not in a bad way, wants to know who is getting paid what every time he makes a decision about who to hire. If that guy gets paid more, *that's not the guy.* This is all the criteria he needs.

The second guy could be 100 times better at his job, but my uncle is not concerned about that. He's concerned about cost alone. He would go to two heart surgeons and say, "Okay, you want $50k, you want $75k? I'm going with the $50k option." Half of $50k doc's patients are dead, but oh well.

This is the scarcity mindset that I still see with some advisors I employ here: *if someone else is succeeding, that's somehow detracting from what I'm doing.* It's a zero-sum approach.

I'm pretty well known for my guerrilla videos (shot on an iPhone for that extra terrible and shaky look) among my peers. Sometimes they will ask me, "Aren't you afraid your clients are going to see those videos and feel like you're living too high on the hog?" Because I'm always somewhere, Guatemala, Croatia, whatever. My reply is always, "No, I don't have scarcity clients. My clients don't believe that because I'm somewhere else, or because I'm on vacation, their returns are going to be worse." That's just naïve. Really, it's just stupid. My clients, in fact, encourage me: "Where'd you go? What'd you do?" Because that's what I do for them. Everybody gets lifted up together.

I don't like doing business when I don't feel like everyone's winning. Doing business in the late 1980s, I could say, "Look, here's the deal," and you'd say, "That seems pretty good, how about this or that?" and I'd agree. We'd shake hands and that would be the deal. It was a win-win.

Now, people do not do business like that. Now they're never satisfied. They've been taught that unless you destroy the other person, it's a bad deal. Today, everybody's going into the conversation with an all-or-nothing mentality. "I'm going to need a little more of your cake," is the thinking right now. And, "Let me have that frosting. You don't really need that fork." So, you're left with a crumb.

This approach breeds one thing: bad service, because you've just taught the person you're doing business with that you don't value what they do.

I want to empower people. I want people to feel comfortable providing me a higher level of service. Don't get me wrong, I want my fair share...but I don't need theirs, too. Some people say it's not personal, it's business. But I say, "It's all personal to me."

I had a meeting, literally yesterday, with a prospect, a soon-to-be client I hope, and he said, "How do I pay you?" I said, "We'll figure that out later, I'm not worried about that." He replied, "Just so you know, I want you to be compensated well. Because I know that will cause you to take good care of me."

So, what I'm getting at is accumulating wealth is just the opposite of what most people think. It's not scrimping and saving. It's building, growing, and empowering the people on your team, and in your life. This guy sees everyone he does business with as his potential ally and another set of eyes to look out for him. I suggest you do the same. This guy is worth $10 million.

He said, before I even asked for anything, "I want to make sure you're fairly paid. Because when I push back or I want something, I want to be comfortable I deserve it and you're being compensated." The result of this attitude is everybody feels good.

If he calls me on Tuesday at 4:00 PM and says, "I need you to come out at six, I've got an emergency," I'm not going to think, "Well, I don't make any money off this person, I'm just going to make up a reason why I can't go." I'm going to make damn sure I drop what I'm doing and go help him.

Most people do not think that way, and it's really a shame.

When I go into Bob's Sunoco to take my car in, I say, "Bob, make sure it's safe, make sure the tire tread is good, make sure the brakes are okay." If he tells me it needs front brakes and four new tires, that's what it gets. I don't question it; I don't say, "Can we get by with two? Are you sure? Let me go call somebody else." I trust him, and I want him to be compensated.

I went into his shop some years ago with one of my cars, and he said, "I think it's the radiator." So, he replaced the radiator. Unfortunately, I got halfway home, and it clearly wasn't the radiator, because the same problem happened again. I brought it back. He called me about two hours later, and said, "You're right, it wasn't the radiator, it was…whatever." He said, "I'm taking the radiator off. I'm not charging you for the brand-new radiator or the labor." Now, that probably cost him $400 or $500, but I've been his customer ever since, without question.

The Abundance of Surrender

Another example of scarcity versus abundance thinking is found in two clients I've had over the years, two doctors. Same practice, same income, same whitecoat, same microscope and the same desire to be financially successful. Guy one would drive me out of my mind. He always wanted to know why this was up, and this was down, and why does that cost that?! The other guy, he would just write me a check, and say, "Don't bug me." This went on for years.

Guy number one, his net worth was probably somewhere in the $700,000 or $800,000 range. He spent his entire investing career scrutinizing every dime, every turn in the market, every geopolitical issue, every election. It was always something. Guy number two ended up worth $5 or $6 million dollars. This guy, he went skiing and traveled the world. This is not to say you should be ignorant. But it's worth considering how you spend your energy A) in life, and B) in investing. Somehow, trusting and letting go seems to work. I can't exactly explain why, it just does.

People choke the life out of the process. They overthink everything.

I still have this issue in the advisors I employ. I have advisors who are $2.5, $3 million producers, and I have $200,000 or $300,000 producers. The $200,000 guy, he'll spend a month researching a stock. The $3 million guy? He's playing golf. With his client.

Guy number two is trying to understand what his client cares about. Many folks would make fun of the golf thing or make fun of the advisor going to an event with a client, but the truth is, this is how you get to know people—get them out of the sterile office environment and really see what they are about. Trust me, most nights I'd rather be home with my family than eating another rubber chicken, but this is an important interaction for both advisor and client.

By the way, guy number one, the $200,000 producer, will never get the stock thing right.

Again, the first guy will never get it. He's choking the life out of the process. My uncle is another classic example. He has that engineer mindset, a certainty person: two plus two always equals four, and if it doesn't, the certainty person will do that math over and over again until it does. In investing, two plus two will *never* equal four. It equals five sometimes, it equals negative two, it even equals 14 once in a while. This is the randomness of investing-slash-life.

I understand people want to have absolute knowledge; they're just barking up the wrong tree when it comes to investing.

Key Chapter 1 Takeaways:

- You can't predict the future.
- Value your time.
- Empower others.
- Make a decision without agonizing over every detail.
- Embrace an abundance mindset.
- Stop believing in scarcity. 2 + 2 does not always equal 4.
- You can't have absolute knowledge when it comes to money or investing.

I've Never Made Anyone Rich

Chapter 2
I Don't Make Anyone Rich

"Time is more valuable than money. You can get more money, but you cannot get more time." ~Jim Rohn

How to make a million? As the old and now not-so-funny joke goes...start with two. After 36 years in the investment business, I am still perplexed when potential clients come into my office with the impression it is my job to make them rich.

I've got news for you: if I knew the secret formula for making average folks wealthy in a short period of time, the first guy I would share the secret sauce with is yours truly.

The reality is, in my aforementioned 37 years in "the business" I have never *made* anyone rich. In fact, I probably know 50 financial advisors personally and I am pretty sure not one of them has ever made anyone rich. Now, I know it is conventional wisdom to mistrust advisors and the financial industry on the whole, but effortless wealth creation was never in the job description, and I suggest if your person claims it is, move on.

Folks who are "rich" are that way first and foremost because of something *they* did—not something an advisor, accountant, or attorney did for them. Whether you are a doctor, lawyer, business owner or inventor, the wealth you do or do not have is a direct result of your own doing. In fact, most wealth, I find, comes from years of hard work and a dedication to saving and responsible behavior.

That's right...no secret sauce! I know, I'm bummed too.

My experience has been that money earned and ultimately saved is the norm rather than the exception. Sure, occasionally we see an inheritance, but as I said, most of our successful clients have built their wealth through hard work and dedication to responsible behavior. It is for this reason that the worst thing any financial professional could do for a successful individual is to undo that philosophy.

Why would someone who has worked for 30 years to save a sizable nest egg through frugality and long-term discipline suddenly turn that money over to someone whose whole pitch is the exact opposite of what got them there? In short, *if it ain't broke, don't fix it*. I am not saying you should not invest, nor am I saying a moderate and well-thought-out strategy and/or process that has some risk is not appropriate. What I *am* saying is buying the "hot" product or security is completely counterintuitive to the behaviors that established your nest egg in the first place.

Saving a million bucks over thirty years and then trying to double it over the next two will generally have the opposite result.

A quick word here about inheritances: If you're thinking of leaving your children lots of money and believe you're doing them a favor, make sure they're educated in terms of what to do with that money before you go. I see a lot of 50-year-olds who are literally sitting around waiting for their parents to die. Not in a morbid, mean-spirited way...but what I see is that they're not doing anything professionally because they know that when their parents die, their finances are going to change dramatically.

The problem with this is they're not equipped to handle it. If they haven't worked hard enough to make their own money and been diligent about saving, they'll have zero respect for that money when it shows up. It's not that they will *intentionally* squander it. No. They will unintentionally squander it because they haven't been taught the value of the money. So, I don't think you're doing your kids a favor if you create a situation where they don't have to be responsible for their own well-being and their own financial outcomes prior to your passing.

The Woman in the Red Dress

I hate to admit this, but I'm that guy. I'm that one guy who never saw the classic movie *The Matrix*. Over the years, I have heard folks refer to the film repeatedly, having to nod along as if I had a modicum of a clue as to what they were talking about. It is for this reason that on my most recent lengthy overseas flight, I finally decided to – once and for all – end my tenure of Matrix ignorance.

Now, most of you are familiar with the story, but for the few who (like me) avoided it intentionally or accidentally, it is a film that exploits the gnawing feeling we all have that we are living in some sort of controlled universe – parallel to and separate from – true reality. Not unlike *The Truman Show*, but darker.

In this parallel universe, people live under the false impression they live lives of free will and self-determination, when in fact, every aspect of their existence is planned and manipulated by machines. In short, they are being placated by a series of false and superficial distractions designed to keep them content and, more importantly, compliant. First, let me say the film was decent and held my attention even though I will never be able to watch Keanu Reeves (Neo) without thinking of Ted of *Bill and Ted* fame. In the film, Reeves' character Neo has been identified by Lawrence Fishburne's character (Morpheus) as "The One," meaning Neo is capable of outwitting and outgunning the Agent Overlord (the machines) and ultimately freeing all of humankind from the shackles of a false existence.

This is the time, as with all of my musings, that you may be losing patience and wondering how I'm going to tie the review of a 20-year-old movie into our world of wealth accumulation and maintenance. As always...hang on. You see, investors like Neo are tested early and often. In what could be described as his "Training Phase," Neo is put through a series of tests and simulations, one of which involves the infamous "Woman in the Red Dress."

In this scene, Neo moves through the somewhat bland and hypnotic gray and white world that is the standard manipulated human existence when he is suddenly distracted by a woman in a bright red dress. This woman is an intentional distraction designed by Morpheus to illustrate how humans are easily placated by things that address their simple need for a short-term solution or satisfaction. In my mind, the red dress is akin to the short-term dopamine release we get when engaging on social media, partisan politics, or our phones when we are faced with even a moment of potential boredom.

For our purposes, the "Woman in the Red Dress" comes in many forms. The machines have figured out that things like crypto, meme stocks, day trading and the "next big tax avoidance secret" are just enough of a distraction to keep you spending in the short term and *away* from focusing on the long term. She's that glance at your phone while driving or that impulse to sell off your quality stock portfolio to buy the new crypto your son-in-law says "can't miss." The Woman in the Red Dress is as she was for Neo, not real.

She was designed to distract and satiate. She is not interested in your long-term success but merely in distracting you for the benefit of the machines.

The machines also come in many forms: politicians, get-rich-quick YouTubers, influencers, large trading platforms, can't-miss real estate deals, currency scams and Nigerian princes in need of a short-term cash infusion. The machine could be your obnoxious in-law who swears he can turn your ten grand into twenty grand overnight...or it could be a giant investment firm suggesting that their trading platform with pretty blinking lights is not just a dopamine hit, but all that stands between you and eternal happiness.

My job, as I see it, is akin to that of Morpheus. Together, we must always remain vigilant and wary of the "machines" and their self-serving need to feed off our impatience and propensity for short-term and superficial dopamine hits. Dopamine, the neuro-modulatory molecule that makes up that warm fuzzy feeling we get when something pleases us, is often a short-term buzz with negative long-term consequences.

Consider reading this book as part of your ongoing training and a reminder that the machines are everywhere. They are pointless political dogma and shiny can't-miss opportunities. They are gambling sites and media-based "enrage and engage" ad sales tactics. For the most part, the machines want you to be complacent and easy to manipulate. They want you to expect wealth accumulation (and even life) to be easy, thus making you eager to buy parallel solutions that are not reality.

Those who expect the journey to be hard yet rewarding will never become stuck in the Matrix.

If You're Lost, Pull Out of Traffic

When it comes to getting where you want to go financially, people should just step aside for a minute. Pull out of traffic, so to speak, and admit to yourself, "Okay, I've been doing this for 20 years, and I've been wary of advisors and wary of investment people and wary of this and wary of that, and I've been thinking everyone's out to get me..."

Everyone is not out to get you. They're making a living, just like you are.

Take a minute to say, "Okay, this mindset isn't working. My net worth was $50,000 ten years ago, and now it's $75,000. I am not where I want to be, and this situation isn't changing fast enough."

The numbers I'm using here are admirable, and for some people even fantastic because they just have limited means. But to most people, a net worth of $75,000 isn't "rich," and if you obsess about clipping coupons (and only that), then you're never going to get where you're going. If you say, "I've been doing this and it's not working, I'm still not comfortable!" I think you must reevaluate. Take a second job. Ask yourself, "The time I sit in front of the TV, could I take that two or three hours and drive Uber? Could I take that time and work at Walmart? Or do I take that two hours and take a course? Do I go back to school?"

You might be thinking, *I'm 50, I'm not going to go back to school!* Well, how old will you be if you *don't* go back to school? I remember reading about a woman who graduated from college at 92. When she went back, people were saying, "How old are you going to be when you get out?" She replied, "Well, how old am I going to be if I don't go back to school? What difference does it make?"

Go back to school and become a physical therapist, or find some passion that you like, or take a financial class—just better yourself as a human being. Whatever it is, it's more profitable than the clipping of the coupons, and more likely to enhance your wealth.

As I've mentioned, finding a good financial planner is worth its weight in gold. Like gold, finding a good planner is most difficult. Most folks call the local "big brokerage" or use the advisor their parents used. Sometimes this works; most of the time it does not.

My recommendation is to find the least assuming, most prosperous person you know and ask her for a recommendation. Conspicuous consumers who "appear" to have it made are not your go-to. Find the person who drives the old F-150 or Camry (see *The Millionaire Next Door* by Thomas J. Stanley and William D. Danko) who also gives to charity and has a nice but modest place in the mountains. That's your gal. Thoughtful people gravitate toward professionals who are cut from the same cloth.

The guy driving the Ferrari with not much in the bank will likely gravitate toward the same type of person. Again, my experience is that most "financial advisors" are a bad quarter away from getting their Porsche repossessed. Find someone who is willing to sit down and develop a game plan and a budget.

Most advisors will find a way to wiggle out of this, because WHY, CLASS? Hey, you in the back slobbering on the desk...BECAUSE THEY DO NOT GET PAID TO DO THIS! They get paid to get your money on the books. My suggestion is to ask an advisor you are considering working with what they would charge to build you a detailed track to run on, and if it's not crazy, pay it. This means they are being compensated for their time and expertise, and you will feel comfortable complaining if the path looks more like a dirt road than the "Yellow Brick Road."

Where to Begin

When you're just starting out in this project, don't make it about investing. If you make this about investing, especially early on, you're going to get in your own way. Make it about saving. If you turn 50 and you've only got $1,000 saved, I don't give a crap how good you are at investing, it isn't going to matter. So, save. You're going to have a year where you earn zero—plan on it.

Once you get that process in place, that discipline built in, whether it's $10 a month or $1,000, then you can worry about investing. Because if you have $100 and you double it tomorrow, you still can't retire! You have to save first.

The questions I get all the time are, "What's the best fund? What do you think the market's going to do?" I always respond, "Well, how much are you saving?" If I hear, "I haven't started yet," I'm not answering those questions!

The biggest crime that's perpetrated on people by my industry are headlines like, "THE BEST TEN FUNDS FOR 2019." How about, *just save*. Those funds, first of all, aren't going to be the best funds again. Don't get caught up in the hype.

Just stop. Just save.

The Life-Changing Magic of Personal Accountability

Let's look at the success or lack thereof in your financial planning. You see, for many, if not most, of you, the reality is *there is no planning*. There is simply hoping. Hope, of course, is what gets us all out of bed each day and drags us to the coffeemaker. Hope is what drives us to educate our children and contribute to our community.

Hope, however, is not a plan. Hope on its own, lacking a plan, is what causes you to buy lottery tickets. Hope without a plan is what leads people to make terrible financial decisions every day.

"I hope this guy offering a 20% guaranteed return is not gonna be the subject of an *American Greed* episode next year."

"I hope that my parents don't spend all my inheritance on that trip to Africa."

"I hope that my financial advisor can double my money with no risk."

Hope, hope, hope. My father used to have a saying about hoping in one hand and shitting in the other and waiting to see which one filled up first. Funny dude, my dad.

What I'm trying to say is: it's time. It's time to stop. It's time to take control of your financial future. It's time to stop pointing fingers at everyone and everything else and look hard at the man or woman in the mirror. I challenge all of you who are on the "hope" program to pair your hope with a good and actionable plan. Democrats don't keep you from saving and neither do Republicans. The president didn't make you buy that car you can't afford, and the Speaker of the House did not tell you to go out to dinner every night. ENOUGH, I say!

Start with a real resolution, one you can actually accomplish. Don't tell me you're going to save 50% of your income...cause you ain't! Tell me you're gonna pay an extra $100 per month on your mortgage or eat out two fewer times per month and put that money in savings. Tell me you're gonna stop paying for cable stations you haven't watched in five years (seriously, STARZ?).

Wall Street is not your problem, politicians aren't your problem. *You* are your problem.

Sure, it's hard to save. I get it, but as I often say, "If it's the easy way, it likely isn't the right way."

Financial freedom, to borrow a phrase, is not complicated; it's just hard because it requires discipline and humility. If you are looking for someone to blame, scapegoats are easy to find. Politicians, greedy corporate types, black cats and homework-eating dogs are plentiful. Maybe this is the year you stop looking for scapegoats and start looking for a plan.

This, I proclaim, is the year of the no-excuses financial plan for you and your family.

Inner Locus of Control

You are in control of your outcomes. I understand this idea can be tricky. The truth of the matter is some things are out of your control. If you get hit by a car, that's probably out of your control, right? But what will you do *after* you get hit by a car? There are millions of stories of people who've overcome hardship, who have come from bad places, from poverty, from war zones, people who have lost limbs, people who've gone through all *kinds* of adversity and come out stronger – because they refuse to accept that the world is going to dictate to them their outcomes.

Yet when it comes to financial outcomes, there is no shortage of people who say, "Well, my financial outcomes are poor because someone else did something," or, "Things are bad because this political person I don't like is now in office," or "inflation got me," or, "my boss was mean to me." These are all outer locus descriptions, and people who have an outer locus of control far and away underperform people who have an inner locus.

People who say, "I don't care what you throw at me, I am responsible for my own outcomes," tend to do well. They say, "*I will dictate to the world how my life is going to turn out.*" And they do. Of course, we all have days where we feel sorry for ourselves. We're allowed those moments. But the inner locus person analyzes, absorbs, and moves on.

Consider Raising Your Income. It's Your Decision.

I've been thinking about making a documentary about Uber drivers because I use Uber a lot. I think it's the greatest thing ever. For everyday working people, it's hard for them to get ahead and find the money to even begin investing. They will spend a Saturday clipping coupons to save $50, maybe, and it's significant, don't get me wrong. But if they took that same Saturday and drove for Uber, they might make $500.

Many folks are so convinced that this micromanagement of expenses is the secret, which I think is a nefarious thing corporate America has convinced people: *Spend your time looking for the better deal.*

What if instead, for example, you started a lawn business, and every other Saturday you cut grass? You might make a few hundred bucks or even more.

It hit home for me when I was riding with this Uber driver recently. I was going downtown for something, and I always talk to our drivers. It drives my wife crazy, but I want to understand what they're thinking, so I ask, "What do you do, do you normally work this day?" Et cetera, et cetera. This guy was an immigrant from Cameroon. He was dressed to the nines, his car was impeccable, and he lived in Sebring (70 miles from Orlando, where I was picked up). He worked at the penitentiary during the week. On weekends, I learned he gets in his Suburban, drives to Orlando and Ubers for 24 hours. I asked, "Why do you do that?"

He replied, "I can make almost the same amount of money as my day job, and I literally almost doubled my income by working for Uber on the weekend."

Most people would never ever consider that. They would rather drive across town to grocery store B because grocery store A is twenty cents more expensive, or shop for a car for three or four weeks. I would argue, for some Americans, there is value in that. But I would also argue it makes sense for those people to get a part-time job or work for Uber or whatever. Freelance. Get a side hustle.

Our education system, I could go on for a novel on how our education system trains us to do these stupid things. We're taught to be employees and we're taught to *spend* money well, not *make* money well, not how to be business owners. Our high schools and colleges are immensely broken institutions that have not changed in 100 years or more. Go sit in a desk in a stale classroom and listen to a professor drone on and on about something inane that more than likely will be of no use to you beyond tomorrow's episode of *Jeopardy*? I think we can do better, and some schools, some programs, *are* doing better. It's just not the norm yet.

Our schools are designed to make us good employees and, less overtly, good consumers. Have you ever been to a job fair at a college? You know the ones. Each giant Fortune 500 company has its own booth with enormous logos and a really sharp looking recruiter. In their own way, they probe you and evaluate you the way a beef buyer looks at a cow before slaughter: "Hmm, nice teeth, good verbal skills, and no detectable odor. This one will fit nicely in our technology department where we will pay her just enough to over-consume and get buried in debt to the point where she can never leave, but will fall short of total financial annihilation. Yes, this one will work nicely."

Schools teach young people to be obedient and avoid, at all costs, the financial education that would free them from the indentured servitude most find themselves stuck in. Fortunately, I think this dynamic is changing a little bit. Younger people are starting to tune into the key ideas: *Maybe I can be my own boss,* and *Maybe I don't want to be a millionaire, but I can control my life.*

I have clients and my clients are my bosses. But my clients also respect me. Sometimes I will get a call, because some of my better clients have my cell phone number, and if they call on a Saturday or a Sunday or late at night, they'll say, "Scott I'm really sorry, and I promise I'm not going to do this again, but…"

That's all I need to hear. I'm quick to answer the question or fix whatever they need.

I Don't Make People Rich, and Neither Does the Lottery

Seriously people, stop buying lottery tickets. Number one, you are not going to win. The odds of winning the Powerball jackpot are 1 in 292 million, and these odds never change.[4] Two, that money could go to a good cause, like buying my breakfast occasionally at the local diner. Three, I went to get my Xanax (kidding) prescription filled at the grocery store last week and the whole darn town was in a line that went all the way back to the ice cream counter and blocked the beer aisle to boot.

The lottery pisses me off. The lottery is illegal for anyone but the state to run, and many experts see it as a tax on addicts. Why? Because more than half of American adults play the lottery occasionally but only a small percentage of those players account for most of the sales. According to one report, 54% of lottery sales come from only 5% of players.[5]

The state, the government, will tell you gambling can only be here or there, and we don't want people behaving in a poor fashion, and we don't want them paying fees on 401(k)s, but we'll let them throw away $100 a month on lottery tickets that will get them nowhere. I'm truly not anti-government, but this is baloney!

Why is this? You might ask. I'll tell you why—we can't balance our state budgets and this is a cheap and easy cheat our politicians have developed.

We also know, statistically, that the people who've played the lottery the most are the people who can afford it the least. We

---

[4] wired.com/2016/01/the-fascinating-math-behind-why-you-wont-win-powerball/ Accessed December 2017.
[5] http://govinfo.library.unt.edu/ngisc/reports/lotfinal.pdf Accessed December 2017.

know that. The same people who are sent a Social Security check that they're living on for $1500 are spending $300 of it on lottery tickets, and then calling to complain because their check's not big enough.

The lottery was illegal throughout the United States until 1964.[6] I'll never forget, as long as I live, the day the lottery started in Florida. I was on my way to an appointment, I needed gas, and I walked into the 7 Eleven. The line to buy lottery tickets was *out the door*. None of the people in that line looked like they could afford it; a lot of them were elderly. The lottery pissed me off from Day One, because I couldn't pay for my gas and I knew these people couldn't afford it. This was probably in the late 1980s.

It takes every ounce of restraint I have, because I know it's a pointless conversation, not to say anything when I'm standing behind someone at a convenience store who is buying ten or fifteen lottery tickets. They've got their little plastic bag they keep their stuff in, and their information—you know, all the "numbers," grandkids' birth dates and the like that are must-play can't-miss numbers. I just want to say, "Why don't you take that ten dollars and save it every week? Then, in ten years, you might have $50,000." Even if someone *does* win (you won't!), about 70 percent of people who suddenly receive a windfall of cash will lose it within a few years, according to the National Endowment for Financial Education.

Again, it's shortcuts. People are always looking for shortcuts.

The lottery is a crime.

---

[6] irp.wisc.edu/publications/focus/pdfs/foc124b.pdf Accessed December 2017.

Rich People Often Have Humility

During the years I have been at this business of money, I have been asked numerous times, "What personality trait would you say is most common in people who are rich?"

The answer is, and I suspect always will be, HUMILITY.

Furthermore, I would point out that the folks I know that you might call rich, I would call successful. The term "rich" to me conjures up images of the Monopoly guy or Scrooge McDuck.

We all know rich people; it's the guy who sends his food back three times and then leaves a 5% tip to teach the poor kid who does not work in the kitchen and is trying to eke his way through college "a lesson."

It's the clown in the high-end sports car who thinks the breakdown lane is his personal avenue when traffic is snarled, or parks his car sideways in three spaces at the grocery store. While I'm sure there are female examples of this, I'm not brave enough to point them out. But the ladies, I am sure, could.

My point is not to pick on the rich, but to point out that, to me, there is a difference between rich and successful.

Warren Buffett is successful; the aforementioned Scrooge is rich. Warren Buffett is giving his money away to help cure diseases in developing countries; Scrooge is swan diving into gold coins. My neighborhood is a haven for the successful and humble-yet-prosperous. We still open doors for one another and wait patiently as the other driver passes by on our often-crowded streets.

Humility is a trait of the curious and thoughtful. Those who know everything generally fail to learn from their mistakes and miss opportunities to grow their investment knowledge. In 37 years, I have been taught more than a few lessons. Things I was sure of turned out to be completely false. Today, I understand that nothing is certain and that what makes sense today may seem idiotic tomorrow. Past truisms include: "Real estate can never go down," "In three years, gold will be the only currency," "Facebook is a can't miss IPO," and of course, "For the last time Copernicus, the Sun revolves around the Earth." (Talk about arrogance.)

For sure, there are people who are not humble who have lots of money and might be what you call rich. My experience, however, tells me that while they may be rich, their lack of humility will, in many cases, be their undoing. Again, I realize there are jerks out there we (or at least some of us) idolize. We watch their reality shows and are mesmerized by their tabloid-worthy lifestyles. In the end, however, if the rest of us don't exercise some discretion and thoughtfulness, then, as the Beatles put it, "Instant Karma's gonna get you."

And even if it doesn't, the securities markets might.

Wonder

Do you ever wonder? No, seriously, do you ever wonder? That's it, end of question.

Most people, I would argue, do not. Most people spend a lifetime being uncurious (yes that's a word). The uncurious established their views on all things political, religious, social and financial (you know, the important stuff) somewhere around their early twenties and spend the rest of their lives confirming those under-informed views. I mean, what did you know at 21? I'm gonna go with NOT MUCH! Looking back on 21-year-old Scott Brown I would say, NOTHING! I knew almost nothing. Sure, I knew right from wrong (mostly), I knew the value of hard work and most definitely the value of a quart of beer at the local pub every Tuesday night, but not much else. My opinions on the intricacies of human interaction and the many challenges of my family, town, and/or country were largely unimportant and completely lacking in any real intellectual effort.

In short, I was an idiot.

Now sure, some of you are right now questioning my use of "was." Both my wife and my children are likely biting their tongues, too. That said, many folks get so busy they take intellectual shortcuts. They rely on headlines and memes (that's the Facebook thing, right?) to confirm their views rather than make themselves uncomfortable with information that may shed a negative light on the view they already hold.

They dismiss headlines without question that are counter to their existing beliefs and copy, paste, and send mentally or sometimes literally (stop it!) the ones that confirm their existing biases. I recently read somewhere that less than 20% of Americans have even read one book in the last twelve months. Truth be told, folks are busy and I get that, but I do not accept it. I guess it's easy for me to judge because I have always been a reader and likely always will be. In my office, we have readers and nonreaders. Much to the nonreaders' chagrin, I constantly bombard them with information I have read and try to reduce it to bite-size portions so they might accidentally learn something.

"In my whole life, I have known no wise people who didn't read all of the time." ~Charlie Munger

Like politics and other fun (read: divisive) subjects, the press does a wonderful job of working your financial bias and short attention span. It doesn't matter whether you like stocks or you hate stocks, there is a headline that will confirm your existing bias. The problem is, you should be reading the one that disagrees with your current position—not just nodding hypnotically at the "ANNUITIES SUCK" headline just because you believe annuities...well, suck. Maybe they do, maybe they don't. Either way, you won't know any more than you did ten years ago if you don't attempt to find out why this is or is not true.

The truth is...there is more than one truth.

Make sure the truth you are confirming is indeed yours and not that of some idiot 21-year-old seeking cheap beer and oysters, because that dude was fun, but he was also broke.

We have all heard and used the terms "20/20 hindsight" and/or "Monday morning quarterback." Essentially, these two clichés are a reference to the fact that every decision seems clear with the benefit of having seen the outcome. "Well, of course my football team was going to lose; clearly they have a quarterback issue and the coach is bad at clock management."

The day before, that same person was explaining how his team could not lose and, in fact, the coach was likely the next coming of Bear Bryant. I could have told you that real estate was going to fall apart in 2007. I mean, come on, it was painfully obvious. Which is why I bought three properties that year. On and on and on it goes. Everybody is a genius the day after. I knew I should have bought

Apple back in 1995! Um, NO YOU DID NOT! If you had known, you would have done it. Period. End of sentence.

Seriously, just stop it...I mean right now.

You did not know then, and do not know now, what is going to happen in markets, sports, entertainment trends, and political theatre. If this year does not prove that we live in a turbulent, unpredictable world, then you, my friend, are spending far too much time in a Colorado dispensary. Let's try to refocus on what we can understand and, more importantly, what we cannot.

Some of you get it (congrats); many of you do not. Investment firms and Wall Street vendors want you to believe three things:

1. Financial outcomes are based largely on picking the right stock, bond, mutual fund and/or like product.

2. The product you should pick and subsequently buy can be determined by looking at its prior performance.

3. They have that product and know what the years ahead are likely to look like.

NO, no and NO! According to a recent study of the top performing 25% Large Cap Products, which totals 198 funds (Blue Chip type stock stuff), less than 5% were able to repeat that performance, and more than half failed to remain in the top half of performers. In short, if a hundred of you bought an investment product sold to you based on the premise it had been a top 25% earner, these would have been the outcomes: less than 5 of you would have had the performance repeated as sold. Around 11 of you would have been slightly disappointed. A little more than 26 of you would have been annoyed and 58 of you would be ticked off.

Now you say, why would anyone buy something based on prior performance? We all know better. *DO YOU!?*

Thirty years of discussing this tells me you do not. Investment product sales companies (yes, that's what they are) know you are lying. Today, when you're in the line at the grocery store, put down the *Enquirer* (yeah, I see you) and pick up *Money Magazine*. Flip through the pages until you find an ad for an investment product that did not do well last year (I'll wait).

Oh, are you done? No luck? SHOCKING! You see, the only ads you will find are for things that did well last year or over the past few years. Be advised that these firms understand you are lying when you say you do not or will not chase returns despite all the evidence suggesting it is a fool's errand. You do and you will. So, what to do now?

STOP IT!

My advice to you is: you *should not* chase and you *should* plan and save. In my opinion, the best thing to do is buy quality investments and hold them hard and fast through the inevitable rough periods in order to help harvest the bounty that is long-term process-driven investing. You should not buy what did awesomely last year because you now understand: it could be, statistically, a losing idea. Still, more often than not when I have a first meeting with a potential client, they will ask me the following question: "What have your investments returned in the past?"

First of all, that presumes that whatever return the advisor earned and will now share with them is likely to be repeated when they invest in it. Let us all now turn to page one of our hymnal (prospectus) and join me in the gospel: "PAST PERFORMANCE IS NOT INDICATIVE OF FUTURE RESULTS." Can I get an *Amen*?

Sure, you all know that in every investment product you have ever purchased, those words are in big bold print. Yet you choose to ignore them. Why do you ignore them? I'll tell you why: because if you can't judge your future outcomes on past outcomes, what is left? How do we know what our returns are likely to be? For the last time: YOU DON'T!

While I'm the last guy to share a lot of love for regulatory bodies, they don't make companies print that disclaimer because it's not true. It is 100% true. Past performance is almost never repeatable. So, when you go to your local broker and they pull out a brochure touting some really awesome rate of return, there are two questions you should ask:

1. What would you say is the likelihood this investment will earn the same return next year?

2. Can you please show me some of the accounts you have that held that investment last year?

You ask number one because if they say anything other than, "It is not likely," they are either incompetent or lying. (Neither one being optimal for a person you are considering giving a large chunk of dough to.)

You ask number two because some (not all) brokers have a habit of looking up the products with last year's highest returns on them and sharing them, as if the strategy they are now shoving in front of you is one they have always used and not a cherry-picking sales strategy many in the brokerage business are so fond of.

To further dissuade you from hitching your future wagon to yesterday's horses, let's consider the S&P 500, the most used index for investors when trying to gauge overall market performance.

The S&P 500 for the ten years ending December 2014 earned on average 8.55%. Not bad, eh?

So now I will ask you a question: how many times do you think over the last ten years the S&P 500 actually earned 8.55%? You guessed it. NONE. The closest it ever came was in 2007 at 9.13%. Other years included -37% ('08) and 32% in 2013.

I know what you're thinking, "That's a really great story, wise guy. How exactly am I supposed to determine what to put my money into?"

Stand by for the boring, all-too-often repeated Financial Advisor Cliché: Put your money into a well-thought-out, long-term strategy that gives you enough risk—and only enough risk—to put you in a position to earn the rate of return that you have thoughtfully calculated you need.

For the last time, stop buying things because of what *they did* and spend more time controlling what *you do*.

Key Chapter 2 Takeaways:

- There's no secret or quick fix to getting rich.
- Take personal responsibility for your level of wealth.
- Consider raising your income on the margins.
- Be humble.
- Stop playing the lottery immediately.
- Don't waste your energy on all the drama of current events.
- Do not chase last year's trends or returns.

Chapter 3
Things the Ideal Client Does

There's a fine line between fishing and standing on the shore like an idiot. ~Steven Wright

I've noticed many of you have your own reasons for not doing things—namely, saving. I read recently that some people think it is in our DNA to be poor savers. That's right, you may have a genetic predisposition to be a reluctant saver. Our ancestors had no reason to save, as the only real currency thousands of years ago was food, and since we had no means of storage (refrigeration, Tupperware, etc.), those who did not eat all they had gathered perished. Subsequently, saving had no value in the days of the cave and club.

Today we face a completely different situation. Not saving is a national pastime, and while savings rates have ticked up in the last few years (from zero), they are still far below the rest of the world.

Did you know that a cup of "fancy" coffee is, on average, more than four dollars per cup? If you made your own coffee every morning and invested that four dollars every day for 30 years at 6% you would have $121,507.00. How about the tub of soda they sell at the local convenience store? How 'bout drinking water and saving that $1.25? That's over $30,000.00 over 30 years at 6%. Smokers: pay attention. At over eight bucks a day, the savings there over the same 30 years at the same rate is over a million dollars.

I used to tell my son he was all about the touchdown dance. To this day, it still pisses him off. What I meant and what I mean by this is many of you have already figured out what you're going to *buy* with your wealth before you've established a discipline for *having* it. In my son's case, he was not much for pushups and wind sprints; he was big on spiking the ball and moonwalking. (Not really, but it is a funny image.)

In the end, saving is not easy and, apparently, genetically not cool. That all said, unless you want to wield a club or live in a cave in your later years, you may want to skip the Caramel Cafe Latte.

The Savers Are Subsidized by the Spenders

If you're like me (poor you), then you have, for the last month or so, been getting bombarded with requests from Apple to update your iOS. If you don't have an iPhone, be afraid; they know who you are. Anyway, the constant requests reminded me that a little over three years ago I wrote a column basically breaking capitalism down to a competition between savers and spenders, winner almost literally taking all.

Now, let me first say to all the lawyers, nitpickers, compliance people, and the 10 or 20 (I lost count) regulatory bodies that can't wait to fine me: THIS IS NOT A SOLICITATION TO PURCHASE OR OWN APPLE STOCK. IT IS MERELY AN EXAMPLE OF WHAT CAN HAPPEN IF ONE SAVES MONEY IN ANY NUMBER OF PLACES VERSUS BUYING CRAP THEY WON'T CARE ABOUT IN 15 MINUTES! Whew.

As I was saying, it is my belief that capitalism can be broken down into those who save and those who spend. Spenders always have, and always will, enrich the savers. Let's look at some real numbers to illustrate this idea.

My example back in 2013 (you're welcome, oh one person who listened to me) was that if you bought $500.00 worth of Apple stock instead of $500.00 worth of Apple stuff (iPhones, watches, etc.) over the previous 10 years, you would have had, at that time, around $60,000.00. The annoying update requests from Apple (which I always ignore for a week or two) caused me to wonder what that number would be today.

So, I checked.

According to Morningstar, AAPL (the stock) is up around 77% since early 2013, or near the time I wrote that piece. Is the point that I am brilliant and if I write about a stock you should buy it? Well, yes (kidding now, very red-faced compliance guy...you guys are so easy).

NO, that is not my point.

Once again, my point is very simple. In this country and other "free market capitalist" (yeah, right) societies, the savers are subsidized by the spenders. If you purchased Apple stock in 2003 as per my original article, today that $500.00 per year investment would now be worth around $108,000. Even if you had started saving the day after my 2013 article, today your $1,500.00 investment would be worth around $2,655.00, which is way better than a sharp stick in the eye or the more likely drawer full of phone or gadget carcasses you likely now have.

Let's take this example further. If you had purchased $500.00 worth of Apple stuff (iPads, iPods, iTouches, etc., etc.) every year for the last 10 you would, as I do, have a bunch of broken multi-colored metal gizmos or the tech graveyard that is our kitchen junk drawer. You would have also spent $5,000 of your hard-earned dollars and received a reward only in the enjoyment/frustration that comes with such gizmos.

If, on the other hand, you had purchased $500 worth of Apple stock each year, you would have well over $60,000 and a nice head start on that Cruise Around the World you and your better half have been talking about for some time.

Americans, at only 5% of the world's population, consume over 30% of its stuff, making us the Kings and Queens of Stuff. The problem with too much stuff is that it can lead to not enough savings in the long run.

Let me address my neighbors who are reading this and tempted to point out some of the gizmos and two-wheeled toys I enjoy in my spare time: to them, I say, "toys are good in moderation." Trust me when I tell you there are lots of cool fishing, riding, and other types of toys I covet as I type this, but I know that, like anything in life, there is a balance—the balance between today's enjoyment and tomorrow's regret.

I often have clients tell me they won't live long enough for it to matter, but I have yet to, in 30 years in this business, have a client get that date exactly right. Twenty years ago, when I used to ask large groups to raise their hands if they knew someone over the age of 90, one or two hands out of 50 might go up. Today that number is close to 25, or half the room. Before you start turning off the air conditioner and, heaven forbid, the cable, life as I see it is meant to be lived. And trust me, I do. Still, maybe the newer iPhone or "I" gadget is okay *not* to have. That money would be better placed in savings for the day when we all have chips in our ears and Apple Logos stamped on our heads.

We all like stuff. Period, end of sentence. Yet we all know that stuff is a bad investment. Don't believe me, ask your friend who still drives that yellow Hummer he (and you know it's a he) had to have back in 2007. How's that bad boy holding its value?

Adding a year delay to each new car, phone, TV, couch, exercise gadget du jour, Beanie Baby, pet rock, purse (oh yeah, I went there) and/or any "must have" consumer good will not cause you to lose your already tenuous social status. What it might do, however, is allow you to add to your for-sure tenuous savings and help your confidence level.

How Do You Handle Pressure?

In the famous Queen Song featuring the now late great David Bowie, the lyrics paint a vivid picture of what being "Under Pressure" can do to a person: "It's the terror of not knowing what this world is about, watching some good friends scream GET ME OUT!"

It seems just yesterday we were basking in the light of a bull market that had no end in sight. Clients would call and say, "I think I'm too conservatively invested," and "Why don't we own more stocks?" Oh wait, that pretty much *was* yesterday. Or, at least a few weeks ago. Funny how the vibe can change in an instant.

As I type these words, the screen in front of me is blood red, and men who were just a few weeks ago valiant slayers of capital markets are now running for their lives. For years, I have been warning of two things. The first of these two things is that you would soon forget about 2008 and the carnage to our collective checkbooks and psyche. Many of you did. The second warning is that you would also react as badly to the next one as you did the last one. We'll see.

Any time the markets dip, some of you will be tempted to call your advisor or push the big red sell button on your trading platform (they make it look so easy on TV, don't they?) Before you do, let me remind you that the biggest traders out there have already sold. They are now waiting for you to do the same so that they can get back in and turn your losses into gains.

"But Scott," you say (which you always do), "Oil is in the toilet and China is pawning Panda bears to make ends meet!" To which I say, so what? Buffett just added to his oil position because he knows $50 oil ain't forever, and the hedge funds know things are cheap and Americans like their things. Stuff (often spelled differently) happens to people.

Successful Clients Have a Plan

A couple of weeks ago, a good buddy of mine was kind enough to invite me fishing over on the west coast of Florida. Early one day, we made our way over to one of Florida's many great line straightening spots, Boca Grande. Let me first say if you have not spent time over in the Pine Island/Boca Grande area of Florida, you are missing out on one of the few remaining "Old Cracker" communities. From the "Tarpon Lodge" which looks like something straight out of a Marjorie Rawlings novel, to the Mangrove-lined streets, you can't help but feel like this was and is Florida at its finest.

Fishing, I also noticed, is a lot like investing. If one boat is catching fish, the other boats will always show up. You want to see a red-faced ticked off fishing guide? Let some yahoo with more boat than brains come roaring up into his school of redfish like an investor flocking to yesterday's headline.

Investors, like fishermen, are trained to focus on what they can see. And what they can see is often the money made by someone else. What a wannabe fisherman sees is the guide reeling in fish after fish, and he wants to horn in on the action. In 1999, it was tech stocks that people watched getting reeled in one right after the other.

"Oh my! Did you see what the Cisco guy just hauled in?"

"Holy cow he's bringin' in 300 shares of Juniper...we gotta get in on this!"

In 2005-08, we watched with envy as dollar after dollar seemed to fall from the sky in the real estate market. Like all good fishermen, many of you showed up at the spot only to find the fish had moved on. The fish you hoped to catch had, in fact, been cleaned and were currently resting in a plate of butter and garlic awaiting the opening of a fine Chardonnay.

What weekend fishermen and their brothers the headline investors always fail to understand is the planning, patience, and hard work that went into the fish they see being caught and the profits they see being made. Our guide got up at five a.m. and ran his boat nearly 30 miles north of us to catch just the right bait. Weekend guy got up at eight, bought some frozen shrimp at Walmart, and hit the water around nine.

My guide would see the fish pushing up half a mile away and run 300 yards in front of them waiting patiently for the fish to come to him. "See 'em?" he'd say. "See what?" I'd say. "There's 300 reds in that school."

Now I gotta tell you, I grew up in Polarized glasses fishing the West Coast. I didn't see squat! (Of course, I lied and said I did to save face.)

Like a good investor, his eyes knew what to look for; mine did not. He didn't drive right up on the fish like an investor chasing tech stocks or oil or gold or...you get the picture. Investors must train their eyes on what others do not see. If it's a headline story, trust me, go fish somewhere else, cuz as they say in Louisiana, "Dem fish done been caught."

Successful Clients Know Two Heads are Better Than One

I once read a study about women investors that detailed the returns that women earned versus their male counterparts in accounts held largely at online firms. What caught my eye was the fact that women outperformed their male counterparts by a good margin on an annual basis, and that they, for the most part, traded a lot less in their accounts. The part that I found most interesting was the section of the article that detailed the returns in joint accounts, and how the design or structure of the joint account was the biggest factor in the success of the account, at least from a return standpoint.

"But Scott," you say, "a joint account is a joint account, is it not?" The answer is no. In some accounts jointly registered with a husband and wife, permission from only one of the registered owners is necessary for a trade to be executed; conversely, in some joint accounts both parties must agree to the trade verbally for said trade to be executed. In short, in the latter case your husband cannot buy stock in Bass Pro shops or the Boston Celtics without your permission; in the former he can.

On with our story. As you might have guessed by my tone, the returns in accounts that require both parties to agree with a trade outperformed the single-party accounts by a decent margin, which leads to the question...why?

Well, how do I put this delicately? Dudes are largely grunting Neanderthals who are into things like man caves and hats that hold beer. Also, what self-respecting man does not own *Caddyshack* on DVD? (Was that delicate enough?)

In fact, I myself love all of these revolutionary ideas, but when it comes to investment success, sometimes *hunt, kill and repeat* does not always serve us men all that well. Like Jerry Seinfeld once said about the remote control, "Women are nesters, they just want to watch TV; men are hunters, they want to see what else is on TV."

Men are, as I am sure you were aware, largely (not always) prone to impulsive decisions driven by their aggressive nature and their need to control outcomes. Unfortunately, outcomes in investing, unlike a wild animal, cannot be outsmarted and then wrestled to the ground. Investment success is largely a matter of patience and thoughtful persistence, something my wife has a ton of and my golf buddies, very little. (300 yards of carry, over water...no problem.)

Before you go calling me a sexist, I recognize that there are exceptions to this rule and we all vary from this description a little

here or there. Still, men often want to tackle and wrestle everything to the ground. They feel that way about their money and their investments. Men are controlling of their environments and they tend to underperform their female counterparts.
Women are more okay with the randomness of life. They'll say, "Why are you getting all worked up about the guy who cut you off?" Or, "Really, you're pissed off about the football game?"

Men struggle with that, on the average.

"What if I'm not married?" you might say. Well, I'm not for gettin' hitched for investment purposes, but finding a thoughtful individual of either sex to bounce ideas off of might be a good alternative. My point...hmm, indeed these are dicey waters I have entered. My point is two heads are better than one. Especially when one of them is wearing a hat with 24 ounces of Malt Liquor pouring from it.

Savvy Clients are Investapreneurs

That's right! I'm making up words now (patent pending).

Have you ever known an entrepreneur? You know, the gal who has decided to work eighty hours per week in order to keep from working forty hours per week? They're an interesting lot, entrepreneurs. They are largely risk-takers and, in many cases, downright fearless. You know the names: Ford, Carnegie, Buffett, Branson, Vanderbilt, and Flagler.

You can see the names of entrepreneurs all over any town on car dealerships, insurance agencies, law firms, restaurants and the like. They were the titans of industry before that job got transferred to bureaucrats. They are the reason the guys in three thousand-dollar suits who fly around in corporate jets exist. The suits didn't build those companies or take the risks that the founders of the companies they now run did; the suits merely push papers around and play polo in the Hamptons.

Sorry, got a little testy there. Where was I?

Ah yes: investapreneurs. Like their cousins the entrepreneurs, investapreneurs take risks and realize they must stick their necks out in order to receive better than average returns.

Nobody likes to be average. If I ask a room full of people to raise their hands if they are above average drivers, 95% of the hands will go up. No offense, but the only good driver in this town is me. If the parked car on the side of the road is on your side, I HAVE THE RIGHT OF WAY...it is not cool to race me to said car and scrape paint off my truck. (You know who you are, lady in the big SUV.)

We all know the average investor in almost every study ever done underperforms the institutions and the indexes in any given year. We know that the reason for this is that they almost always buy and sell at the wrong time. This happens due to their lack of patience and/or courage. It takes tremendous patience and courage to max out your credit cards and risk bankruptcy in order to pay your employees so your new restaurant can survive. It takes amazing courage to start a small business knowing that most small businesses fail in the first two years. It's not like entrepreneurs don't know these statistics; they know them better than most, yet they forge on.

Like successful entrepreneurs, investapreneurs know the statistics as well. They know the average investor has a terrible track record against the indexes and institutions. They know that most investors will buy when things seem rosiest and sell when things seem unsalvageable. In other words, at the wrong times. They know these things and yet they push on.

They know that time and patience are the most likely cure for bad markets. They know that when the pain is unbearable and the stress astronomical it is time to dig deep and focus. These kinds of people reach above average success in business and in investing. In the end, the two are the same.

You may not be an entrepreneur, but you are running a startup called your portfolio. It holds many other companies. Sometimes your little business holds debt and sometimes it holds stocks. Sometimes your liabilities seem insurmountable and your balance sheet looks a little dicey. These are the things business people and entrepreneurs deal with daily. Yet they do not quit and they do not give in. Neither should you.

Key Chapter 3 Takeaways:

- Save.
- Have a plan.
- Don't freak out.
- Be an investapreneur.
- Don't be impulsive about investment decisions.

Chapter 4
What the Misguided Client Focuses On

Better a diamond with a flaw than a pebble without.
~Confucius

I had a client recently call me up a bit annoyed at me due to some recent information he had garnered from a good and "savvy" friend of his. He proceeded to tell me in a somewhat accusatory tone that his friend, over beers (yeah, I also become an expert on many things when I have a "few" beers), had explained to him that his advisor only charged him $125.00 per year to manage his nearly $1,000,000.00. Whoa!? Or is it *WHOA?!*

Anyway, no matter how you punctuate it, the bottom line is that my guy knows ("knows" being the operative word) that I charge him considerably more than $125.00 to manage his somewhat comparable portfolio. In fact, the amount I charge him shows up every quarter like clockwork on his statement as a line item. He went on, in a somewhat belligerent fashion, to ask me why my fees were so much higher—to which I responded, "Cuz I am that much smarter."

After letting him digest my weak attempt at humor, I tried to explain to him that his friend, as "smart" and "savvy" (and inebriated) as he might be, is more than likely a little off in the actual cost of his investments. It never ceases to amaze me how hard people will work at trying to convince themselves of the reality they would like to see, rather than investigate further and accept the reality that is. The reality (without giving you specific numbers—because government regulators are strangely against me telling you things) you should know is that fees are exponentially higher than $125.00 on most, if not all, accounts of six or seven figures.

We can spend another page or two on the inherent value in that or lack thereof, but it does not change the fact that "ain't nobody getting nothing for free" (or $125.00), as my grandfather would say. What blows my mind is here is a dude with a million bucks! That's right, he was smart enough to have a million, but not smart enough to know what he was paying, and worse yet, spreadin' the false gospel to any suds suckin' sucker who would listen. Now, you say (cause you're all cynics), "But Scott, I don't own mutual funds." Listen, I don't care *what* you own, aside from individual stocks that you never trade or a fixed bank instrument; it all costs money, and like it or not, it's generally more than you think.

Don't go getting all huffy with your advisor after you read this. He or she may be providing you a great service that includes numerous things other than money management, not the least of which is keeping you from doing dumb stuff at dumb times. That said, choosing to be willfully ignorant of what you're paying does not prohibit the products you own from collecting their fees. Request your "total" fees from your advisor, and understand that if he or she is comfortable they have earned said fee, they will have no problem
giving that information to you.

Take Care Where You're Putting Your Focus

People should save. Just save. If you have $5,000 saved, I'm not diminishing that, it's a substantial accomplishment for most people. But I'm obligated to remind you that earning 5% or 17% on $5,000 is not going to change your life. Yet consumers with

$5,000 have been *convinced* they should spend every waking hour trying to save on fees and get better returns. When what they should be doing is making more money and saving more money.

When you have $500,000, the difference between 2% and 10% is a substantial amount. Then you have the right to scrutinize returns and fees. But until you get to $50,000 or $100,000, in my opinion, you are wasting your time.

Historically, what I find is people who spend all of their time scrutinizing fees and returns lose in the end. My clients who throw money at me and go, "Scott, I gotta go, try not to get me destroyed here, I'll see you next year," are usually the wealthiest clients. Because they realize there are things they can control and things they can't. They're not going to waste a lot of time on stuff that they can't control.

I just can't impress this on people enough.

Years ago, I drove about 50 miles out to the west coast of Florida to see a new client and look at his annuity. Before you freak out, remember that sometimes there's value in annuities, if you use them for the right reason. As we discussed previously, products aren't good or bad, it just depends on how you use them. Anyway, I said, "Look, you're paying 4% for this annuity, and there's no benefit. There's no living benefit or death benefit; there's no benefit whatsoever coming from that additional cost." Often, people will pay more for an annuity, but there's some benefit for that: guarantees, death benefits, guaranteed income, whatever—he had none of that.

At some point in our conversation, I pointed out to my new friend the cost he was paying and that I could likely provide a similar outcome with a third of the fee. His not-so-surprising response was: "So, you're going to charge me a fee of 1%?" "Yes," I replied. The next response *did* catch me off guard: "Oh, no thanks, I'll just keep the annuity."

As the kids say, "WTF!?" So, you prefer to pay 3% that you *can't* see rather than 1% that you *can* see? Honest to god, I think I went straight to the bar after that one. It turns out some people prefer what they can't see over what they can see, regardless of the cost. "No good deed goes unpunished," as they say. People would rather pay more and not know they're paying more, than pay less and see what they're paying.

People fixate on costs or fees because fees are tangible. Fees are something where they can say, "Make those less." Because they can't say, "Make the market better, make my bonds go up, make GE have better earnings, save for me, make me not have bought that car I shouldn't have bought." It's easier just to say, "Drop my costs, drop my fee."

There's this idea out there: *If I save $200 a year, my life will be great.* Nope. No, it won't. You'll just waste that $200 on something else.

I just want to shake people. Since I can't do that, literally speaking, with this book, I'm doing the next best thing. This question of whether to work with a fee-based advisor or a commission-based advisor is so important. I just want people to understand what they are paying for, how much they are paying, and where it's coming from.

Pattern Seeking: Or, How Your Kindergarten Teacher Ruined Your Investments

From the time most of us were able to speak, and most assuredly since kindergarten, we were taught to seek patterns. In fact, many sociologists would argue that pattern-seeking is in our DNA, and a main reason we have survived this long. For our ancestors, pattern-seeking is the reason they were able to eat and survive and most assuredly, those who could not pattern-seek perished. If your ancestors could not determine where the seeds they planted prospered the most or, even further back in evolution, where the animals showed up each day for a drink of water, they would have died and you would not be reading this.

If your kindergarten teacher had not taught you which shapes made a pattern and your first-grade teacher had not taught you that 2, 4, 6 is followed by 8, you would not have gotten to middle school and most of you would not be where you are today.

Okay, how is this detrimental to your investment success?

Here's how: because you are by design a pattern seeker, you seek said patterns where none exist, and more specifically, you look for them in investments. All of you (I hope) can do 3, 5, 7, 9. Most of you can do 2, 4, 8, 16, 32. The problem is, you try to do that when deciding where to put your hard-earned dollars. Most of you buy yesterday's returns, confusing them with patterns. You assume because an investment in the magazine advertisement earned 8% in 2009 and 10% in 2012 that, indeed, you have sniffed out the pattern and expect 12% in 2013.

I hear pattern-seeking every day from my clients and participants.

It is what led you to buy tech stocks in 2000, to try to flip houses in 2006, and it is what is causing you to worry you are missing the run up in cryptocurrency today (yes—I know what you're thinking). Now, trust me when I tell you, you are not alone. It is this very human trait that investment product marketers prey upon. It is no accident that companies put the returns of last year's best performers in the advertisements. They know your brain's pattern system will overpower your common-sense system. Considering the trillions of dollars now in managed products, I'd say they are right.

In the end, you must exercise discipline and common sense to override your need to seek patterns. The old adage, "Buy low and sell high" exists for a reason. Chasing the returns of yesterday's hot idea will most assuredly satisfy your need to pattern seek, but it will also almost always, in the end, make you wish you had not. My apologies to Mrs. Welch, Rio Vista kindergarten class of 1969.

"They" Do Not Have It Figured Out

When you open your mail this month and pull out your monthly subscription to whatever "Investment Magazine" you favor, I challenge you to find an ad from a mutual fund or investment company touting the worst-performing product they have in their lineup.

Go on, I'll wait...nothing? Hmm? For sure, with all their collective wisdom, Wall Street firms would be responsible enough to nudge their potential customers *not* to the stuff that HAS done well but toward products that have NOT done well as of late, right? You're supposed to "buy low" after all. Still looking? Okay, let's get straight to the point: they don't give a rat's ass about what you buy and the value of said purchase; they only care that you buy something.

A former client (*former* being the operative word here) of mine once told me that he would only give his money to a major mutual fund complex. (Name withheld for fear of being dragged from my bed and beaten in the middle of the night. Let's just say they like the color green and arrows for some reason.) When I asked him why, he said, "They just have the markets figured out." He went on to say that their managers are just the best.

What I am about to point out he did not much care for, as nobody likes to be told their baby is ugly, even if it does look like Richard Nixon. I pointed out to my friend that it would seem to me if they truly had the markets figured out, and if indeed their managers were the best, wouldn't they just have one fund? I mean, his favorite mutual fund complex has over 300 mutual funds. Why 300? If they were as good as he said, wouldn't they just have "THE FUND?" You know, the one they move around to the "BEST" stuff as their collective brilliance dictates? Oh, but you and I, we know the truth.

The truth is they do NOT have it any more figured out than we do. Sure, they are smart, and sure, they do the best they can with the randomness that is our lives and, no less, the markets. But they do NOT have it figured out. They have 300 funds so that when ten or fifteen of them do well, they can advertise those ten or fifteen in the very magazine you are now lining the bird cage with.

Meanwhile, the other two hundred and something funds you are *not* reading about quietly await their turn in the spotlight. Folks, it's all marketing these days (or ball bearings if you're Fletch).

Americans are suckers for a top ten list of any kind, and whether it's the top ten funds or the top ten places to have a hamburger, we can't help but buy into it.

The Stock of the Day Problem

"Google's going to triple," somebody will tell you. Well, that sounds great! How do you know that? "Because so-and-so told me." Well, who's that? "He's my plumber." Is your plumber independently wealthy? Would you say he has more money than you? If not, why are you listening to him?

People just want there to be shortcuts, so they will believe what anybody tells them. I can't tell you how many clients bug me to buy a stock for them. Nine times out of 10, that stock will drop in value or be the worst performer in their portfolio. Not because I'm a genius, but because there's been no research, no thought—nothing went into the decision other than somebody said it.

I had a client recently, a good client and a smart guy, say, "I overheard a conversation at dinner, about a pharmaceutical company, and I want to buy 1000 shares." I had to ask, "Well, first of all, was it, like, the CEO speaking? Because that's insider information, in which case..." "No, no, it was just two guys talking." So, I went ahead and bought the shares for him, and four weeks later the stock was down 50%. I commented, "I guess that ends that experiment." His response was, "Yes." So thankfully, he learned from it, but a lot of people won't. They'll just keep doing it, looking for the shortcut.

It's the equivalent of diet pills. If we could take a pill and all have six-pack abs, wouldn't that be awesome? That's not how it works.

You have to eat a lot of spinach and do a lot of sit-ups, yet nobody wants to do that.

Stop eating candy bars and being pissed off that you're out of shape!

But they will try, and try, and try again...they'll spend 30 years trying shortcuts, where if they would've just bought ten quality stocks, reinvested the dividends, and called it a day, they'd be millionaires.

My industry is terribly good at convincing people they're geniuses. The most recent example is the E*TRADE ads: "If you just get this trading platform, you too can own a yacht with scantily clad women dancing on the deck." It's funny how scarce these ads were while the market was getting crushed just 10 short years ago. Now with markets at all-time highs, folks are ripe for being sold nonsense. Now everyone is convinced it's easy again, but the only person getting the yacht is the guy who owns E*TRADE. It's frustrating for me, but at the same time, it's job security.

Don't Forget to Train Your Planner

Dogs. Aren't they fun? You can teach a dog to do some amazing stuff. Roll over, beg, fetch a paper and, with a little coaxing, bite your obnoxious know-it-all brother-in-law. Back when I was a youngster, house training a dog involved a newspaper and a stern voice. Today training your financial advisor is much the same. Wait...what? You heard me.

Many of you, whether you realize it or not, are "Advisor Trainers." To be fair, many of us are not nearly as smart or as attractive as your Labradoodle, but we are trainable nonetheless. Over the years, my clients have trained me to react to certain situations in certain ways. Often, this training is great. "Scott, we are happy when the market is up and sad when the market is down." Yeah, *that* one even a Dachshund could figure out (no offense to our short-legged friends).

Sometimes, however, what you teach us can work against you.

A client and I parted ways recently and the decision was, for the most part, mutual. This fella had been with me for about ten years when the relationship hit the skids. The reason for our breakup, in my humble opinion, was that he had trained me to be a bad advisor and I had let it happen. In the beginning, he insinuated he did not want to take risks, and that he would be content with returns in the low single digits as long as his portfolio was safe and secure. On the surface, this seems like a money manager's dream scenario. The guy had made it clear he did not want to hit home runs in return for getting home safely.

Got it! Of course, like any prudent money guy, I suggested he would be wise to add some of his hard-earned dough to stocks so as to have a fighting chance against inflation. He reluctantly agreed. In the end, we had a guy with most of his money in boring/fixed income-type stuff and a nominal amount in stocks.

This is where it gets interesting (I swear). My client liked to travel a lot. The problem is that every time he left town, he would call me and berate me into pulling his stock positions out and moving them to cash. Each time for the next year or two, I would argue less and less, thinking he just wasn't cut out for the risk and I should not fight City Hall. Over time, as you might guess, I moved him more and more away from stock-based investments toward those with low volatility and limited upside. My client had taken the newspaper to my nose one too many times and I capitulated.

Here is where the fun part starts. Cut to 2014 and my client starts to get agitated with me again. "What?" you say. "Did you put him back in stocks? Did you get too aggressive and he needed to leave town?" No, no and NOPE! That's right, you guessed it: he was beside himself that he was not keeping up with (drum roll please) the "stock indexes."

My client wanted to know what in the world I was thinking, having him in mostly conservative bond-based investments. The truth is, no recounting of our previous interactions mattered to him. He had taught me that he hated volatility and I allowed that education to influence how I invested his money against my better judgment.

In short, I let the tail wag the dog and we both paid for it. The reality is I'm not sure who is more at fault here, him or me. I tend to think both, but this is for sure a cautionary "tail" (sorry, couldn't help it). If you continue to second guess and beat your trusted partner with the newspaper, expect that advisor to wince when they shouldn't. This is true of any professional in the advice business, whether we're talking doctors or lawyers or financial advisors.

Like a dog, we are trainable. Just be careful what you're teaching us.

Learn to Redirect Your Brain Chemicals Once in a While

If you Google the term "cognitive dissonance," you get a variety of definitions that all more or less lead you to the same conclusion: people like thinking what they like thinking. How's that for clarity? The best example of this is college football fans, in particular

Southern college football fans. As an experiment, let's try an example.

THE GREATEST COLLEGE FOOTBALL PLAYER OF ALL TIME WAS...TIM TEBOW.

Now, if you are anything but a fan of the University of Florida, you are no doubt contorting and wrinkling your nose. What you are *not* doing is considering the logic behind the statement. You are not going through Tim Tebow's resume of accomplishments as a college football player, nor are you then comparing these accomplishments honestly with other like players.

I am certain you are instantly listing in your head ten other players who were better, and the arguments you could make without even considering that the statement above could be right.

This is "cognitive dissonance."

Basically, we as humans forge paths over time that allow the river of chemicals in our brains to run like the Colorado through the Grand Canyon. As "mature" adults, we often struggle to redirect our chemicals. Put another way, it is literally more physically comfortable to think as we have always thought than forge a dam and redirect the chemical river of our minds over a two thousand foot one-million-year-old canyon wall.

Almost weekly as I meet with folks, someone has an opinion on investing that they learned from the media and/or their peers they have trouble accepting as bunk. They sit down in front of me and tell me how they believe they can day trade their way to fortune or that a particular stock that has been in the press lately is a definite can't-miss. They believe this because it is always what they *have* believed, despite compelling evidence to the contrary. Despite the fact that they cannot bring me one person who has become independently wealthy day trading, despite the fact that they cannot show me one stock they have doubled their net worth with, despite the fact that they are clearly full of it, they continue to argue their point without considering that they could be wrong.

My point is not that what you think is wrong, but that most of us have trouble redirecting the chemicals once the discussion moves to the point of defending our position rather than considering the facts. My grandfather always said there are two kinds of people you can talk to: those who listen and those who are waiting to talk.

Those who listen we often call "intellectuals" because they are more comfortable than most with considering two sides of a discussion than the rest of us. Intellectuals include Thoreau, Plato, Aristotle and, of course, Steve Spurrier.

In short, the next time you find yourself in one of those awkward conversations about politics, religion, investing, or (heaven forbid) college football, try to listen and forge a new path in the canyon of your mind. You never know, it might be a more enjoyable journey. In fairness, and to practice what I preach, I have now decided to declare Deon Sanders the greatest college football player to have ever lived. Please excuse me while I get some aspirin.

Key Chapter 4 Takeaways:

- You get what you pay for.
- Train your planner.
- Stop obsessing about the stock of the day.
- There is no "they."
- Take care where you're putting your focus. Save.
- Let go of pattern seeking.
- Learn to redirect your brain chemicals.

Chapter 5
How to Stay Calm in the Chaos

It's been scientifically proven that the less you know, the more you think you know. ~Anonymous

I'm sure people would say, and rightfully so, "You're comfortable, so of course you're not worried about money or about volatility."

Jim Carrey once said, "I wish everyone could be rich and famous for a day, so they could see that it's not what they think it is."

Stuff isn't all it's cracked up to be. It *isn't*. New cars, new motorcycles, new jewelry...none of that crap is satisfying in any way, shape, or form. You see it all the time. The rapper who gets the Bentley, and gets the Rolls, and has $100,000 worth of jewelry around his neck—and then gets arrested the next week? You know, that stuff didn't help him.

When I travel each year, I see people who have nothing. If they're lucky, they have a meal. Yet I see smiles everywhere.

I see how worked up clients get sometimes about some politician, or "I hope the tax thing doesn't come out this way or that way," or "Oh my god, I have to pay capital gains," or "I bought Microsoft and we should've bought Apple!"

Stop it. Let nature take its course. The funny thing is, my clients who are relaxed about money—which is most of them—tend to have more of it. I don't know how to explain that actually, but there is some rhythm to this, and the rhythm is not to get up every day and sweat bullets about markets and wring your hands about everything someone says on CNBC. That is not the rhythm.

What my annual trip to Guatemala allows me to do, when I start to get caught up in the stress—and I do get caught up in it because I'm hearing angst every day from clients, and eventually that's going to have an effect on me—being in Guatemala brings me back down. Watching a 10-year-old with 100 lbs. of coffee on his back laugh at us Americans when he walks by is a reminder. It's a reminder to start the year with a fresh and thoughtful perspective. Money does not control me, and the funny thing is, the folks who it controls the least seem to end up with the most. My mission trip gives me perspective. At the end of the day, I'm still a capitalist and a fairly good one; that said, I need balance and most good investors do, too.

Investing is a rhythm. Long-term investing is a rhythm.

All of it's a rhythm. You have a pattern of saving that you're comfortable with. You have a pattern of spending that you're comfortable with. You have a style of investing that you're comfortable with. Unfortunately, most people never get into a rhythm. It's all fits and starts. *Oh! I saw that on TV. Augh! But the other guy said that. And then my cousin told me about a guy who says you have to buy Bitcoin! Gold! Real estate!* And on and on.

There's no rhythm. It's just this herky-jerky Elaine Benes dance that's going on. It's uncomfortable for them, and for the people around them, and it's also completely ineffective.

Scared people don't make money; scared people hide under the covers until all the best opportunities are gone. Am I saying it's the bull market's over? Heck, I don't know! We've been over this, people. If I knew what the market was going to do, I'd be on my private island sipping a drink with an umbrella in it whilst being fanned with faux palm fronds made of one hundred dollar bills. (I may have thought about that a bit too much.)

On the Pointlessness of Worry

I have noticed, for the last 13 years or so of my career, that folks tend to worry a lot more than they used to, or at least they tend to share their worries with me a lot more than they used to (thanks, by the way). I don't know if it's old age or a certain understanding I've come to after so many years in this business, but I find most of the things people concern themselves with, especially when it comes to investing, are things they have no intention of doing anything about. Or, even if they did plan to do something, they really couldn't.

Many of you know the celebrated "Serenity Prayer" made famous by the mid-20th century philosopher Reinhold Niebuhr: "God grant me the serenity to accept the things I cannot change; the courage to change the things that I can…and the wisdom to know the difference."

I know you know this prayer, and I would bet a high percentage of you have this very quote hanging somewhere in your house. My mother does, and she still has not accepted her inability to change me into a respectable human being.

This brings me to my now long-awaited point: stop worrying about things you cannot control!

I hear all kinds of worry from friends and clients, mostly surrounding geopolitical events and/or domestic upheaval that will eventually lead to some catastrophic outcome. In the end, the thing that gets you is the thing you never saw coming. Know that the things you are worried about politically or economically are not the ones you should fear. In fact, you should fear none since, unless you are running for political office or contemplating a coup of some type (yes, I know some of you are), then as Doc Holiday once said, "There is no normal life, Wyatt (Earp), there's just life; now get on with it." Maybe that was just Val Kilmer as Doc Holliday? Point stands.

I decided, in order to help you with this getting-on-with-it process, to devise a list of things you should and should not worry about:

1. Worry about how much you save.
2. Don't worry about where the President is playing golf (generally Florida).
3. Worry about how much you spend.
4. Don't worry about the National Debt clock (it's gonna spin with or without you).
5. Worry about getting good seats at the ball game.
6. Don't worry about China's currency manipulation.
7. Worry about getting a table at Taco Tuesday.
8. Don't worry about the Fed and whether or not they will taper.
9. Worry about that brutal par 3 at the local golf course.
10. Don't worry about the small stuff. And, as they say, it's mostly all small stuff.

Before you sit down to write me a nasty email accusing me of not caring or being flippant about our country and its many challenges, understand that I do care and, in fact, spend much of my day contemplating the things I just told you not to worry about.

Contemplating an issue with calm reason versus the borderline apocalyptic mindset that the media likes to goad us into are two very different things.

Embrace—Or, At Least Accept—Change

Suppose 18 years ago I told you, "The United States will be hit by the worst terrorist attack in history. We will respond by launching two wars, one of which will go badly and leave Iraq—a country with the world's third-largest oil reserves—in chaos for years. Iran will gain strength and move to acquire nuclear capability. North Korea will go one step further and become the world's eighth declared nuclear power. Russia will turn hostile and imperious in its dealings with its neighbors and the West. In Latin America, Hugo Chavez of Venezuela will launch the most spirited anti-Western campaign in a generation, winning many allies and fans. Israel and Hezbollah will fight a war in southern Lebanon, destabilizing Beirut's fragile government, drawing in Iran and Syria, and rattling the Israelis. Gaza will become a failed state ruled by Hamas; peace talks between Israel and the Palestinians will go nowhere (again)."

My bet is you would have asked me to go to cash in all of your accounts, and probably many of you would have buried that cash deep in your backyard, thinking that economic growth was impossible and that we would all, by now, be driving around in one of those cool car/dune buggy contraptions that were all the fashion in *Mad Max*. The above events, outlined in Fareed Zakaria's book *The Post-American World*, as I am sure most of you know, did happen.

What did not happen was the end of our world, nor anything that resembled a complete economic meltdown (okay, '08 was a bit dicey). In fact, in the seven years following the aforementioned events, Zakaria points out that the World Economy grew at its fastest pace in nearly four decades. Income per person across the globe rose at a faster rate (3.2 percent annually) than in any other period in history.

It seems that many of us were under the impression that the world was just fine 18 years ago and that things should not and would not change. The fact of the matter is that things have and will continue to change. Like any change, the restructuring of the world order can be fraught with growing pains. These days, change seems to come at a furious pace, which makes some of us nervous. This response is both understandable and mostly pointless. Even on my quiet little street, change is afoot as some of our cute little bungalows are being torn down in favor of larger, less humble abodes.

I don't like change all that much myself, but I know it is inevitable and you can either stand around whining about it or learn to prosper from it. Hitting the panic button every time Congress is at an impasse (daily, it seems) is a waste of time. Understand that major market participants are robotic and bent on making money. While you're sitting in your living room glued to every word Wolf Blitzer is spitting out, they are trying to figure out what you will sell in a panic...so they can buy it!

Sleep on It

There was a day, not too long ago when the market was going to heck in a handbasket. The carnage was in the 8% range. I waited for my phone to ring. In my business, good news falls into the "look what I did" category and bad news falls into the "wait till I get a hold of that stupid advisor of mine" category.

Well, it's now 9:55 am and the Dow is down many, many points and the phone still has yet to ring. Is it possible after thirty years of driving home the idea of patience and perseverance that my clients have finally swallowed the Kool-Aid? Is it possible they understand that time in the market is far more effective than timing the market? Is it possible they realize a diverse portfolio with pre-designed disciplines for selling and buying is better than the "I'm getting left behind...oh no, I'm getting killed" strategy employed by most?

Is it possible they now understand the media uses phrases like "upturn" and "increase" when the market is moving up and terms like "plunge" and "crater" when the market is dropping? Nah. It's now 2:00 pm, and the phone has started to ring: people who three months ago were sure they wanted more in equities and less in cash and bonds now want to get completely out of stocks. I mean, I wouldn't be so paranoid if everyone weren't out to get me.

Once again, I cite the Investment Company Institute study (a real page-turner, I might add) from 2011 that shows professional investors (like the ones endowments have) out-earning individuals on average 8.12% to 3.49% from 1992 to 2011. Why? I'll tell you why: they do not chase returns in either direction. They have strict buy/sell disciplines that don't start with, "Holy &%#!, the world is ending! Sell!" Or, "I can't stand being left out! Buy!"

If you don't have a process that involves strict discipline, moments like today will drive you out of your mind and result in mediocre-to-bad returns over time. If you can't tell me right now when you add to your stock and/or bond positions and when you reduce them, you are, for the most part, a chaser. Most people are reactionary versus proactive.

A wise man once said, "If you don't have a process, you don't know what you're doing."

I suggest that when you get your brokerage or 401(k) statement next month and are tempted to do something silly, do as my friend Karl Stuart in Texas advises instead: "I were you, I would take a nap until the feeling goes away."

Relax: We're All Missing Out, All the Time

> *The desire to acquire the good things of this world is the dominant passion among Americans....it is odd to watch with what feverish ardor the Americans pursue prosperity and they are ever tormented by the shadowy suspicion that they may not have chosen the shortest route to get it. Americans cleave to the things of this world as if assured that they will never die, and yet rush to snatch any that come within their reach, as if expecting to stop living before they relish them. They clutch everything but hold nothing fast, and so lose grip as they hurry after some new delight.*

As you may have already figured out, I like to read. Oh sure, I like to read the normal stuff, *People* magazine and the like, but what I really like to read is history. The above passage from Alexis de Tocqueville's *Democracy in America* was written around 1835 after he toured America in hopes of studying and understanding the rise of Western economies.

Our friend Alex was a Frenchman, and we as good Americans would be remiss if we didn't scoff at any conclusions about ourselves gleaned from a Frenchman, so I will pause here while you consider your list of jokes about the French in your head...are you good?

Like I often do while reading history, I started to translate the essence of what de Tocqueville was saying to the investment business and, more exactly, the way Americans tend to go about investing their money. In the passage above, he observes that Americans "are ever tormented by the shadowy suspicion that they may not have chosen the shortest route" to prosperity.

I think this translates quite nicely to the "need" of many investors to get the "best" returns in an attempt to shorten the path to prosperity. It is also the reason some people would rather stand in line to buy lottery tickets for ten minutes than take that same ten minutes to discuss their retirement plan with a professional.

I see a certain fear of being left out in most people who struggle with their finances. Rather than sit down to develop a plan and stick to it, most people fall for the shiny product of the day over and over again. In 1999, it was tech stocks that were gonna "make us rich," in 2005 it was real estate, followed by gold in 2009.

The common factor in all these things we rushed to snatch up was not that they were necessarily bad investments. It's that we don't "hold any of them fast" through the rough patches. We "clutch everything" when we perceive a shortcut and "lose grip" as we hurry onto the next one.

Instead, we need to become comfortable with our own limitations and bad financial habits, and work to overcome the natural tendency to worry that we might be missing out on the next great investment. It's time to accept the often boring and tedious process of trying to accumulate wealth and stop giving in to the idea that if you don't try to earn 20% per year, you will miss out. Because if that's the case, *we're all missing out.*

I suggest you take a cue from the French: get a table at one of our many great outside cafes, have a glass of wine with a friend, and spend two hours planning to get rich slowly. You could ask the waiter to be rude so you can get the total French experience (sorry, couldn't resist).

Consider Your Beliefs

Somewhere around 2000 BC, the Mayans built an amazing and technologically advanced society. From aqueducts to reservoirs and advanced plumbing, by most accounts Mayan society was well ahead of its time. For a few centuries, the Mayans not only thrived but dominated the Central and South American landscape.

At some point, however, the Mayans became victims of their own success. The technology that led to prosperity also led to a growth in population and a strain on resources. Simple needs like water and food soon became difficult to attain; the solutions to new problems became hard to solve. Eventually, the Mayans, like the Romans and other advanced societies, fell back on beliefs when the needed solutions proved complex and largely overwhelming. Soon the need for food was met with the sacrifice of animals—and likely humans—in order to win favor with the gods of produce and the deli aisle.

In investing, almost all we have are beliefs. We believe that the markets will do well and that free market capitalism will work. I also believe these things. Where belief becomes an issue is when we "believe" that we will earn 20% because we *need* that high rate to make up for our lack of savings.

Believing your financial advisor knows which stock will double next year because you have a balloon payment due is not only silly, it is downright dangerous. Believing you can day trade your way to riches and a Ferrari is likely to put you on the same scrap heap as the Mayans. While finances can be complex and daunting, responsible and disciplined behavior are the logical choices that might very well save you from needing to sacrifice any nearby family members at the next reunion.

It Is Always Easier to Be a Cynic. Don't Be a Cynic.

There once was a hot dog vendor in New York City who made, by all accounts, the most delicious hot dogs in Manhattan. People would come from all parts of the city to enjoy his signature chili and kraut dogs. The vendor was not only memorable for his cuisine but also revered for being so good at his craft despite being both blind and deaf. Over many years, the hot dog vendor had built his business along with his son into a New York institution, and as his son was about to leave for college, they had together built numerous locations.

Soon after his son left for college, the hot dog vendor decided to expand his business and began advertising and adding locations to such an extent that his business almost doubled. Now, somewhat because of his physical limitations and more accurately because of his rigorous work schedule, one important fact escaped our hero the hot dog vendor: his city and his country were slowly becoming mired in a devastating recession.

In fact, because business was so good, he hadn't any reason to be aware of the recession or the struggles of those around him. Some months later, his son returned from college, now armed with a deep understanding of the world around him and the difficulties of his city and beloved country. The son, upon learning of his father's recent expansion and advertising campaign, began to implore his father to immediately cease his expansion and cancel any further advertising campaigns.

Being a simple hot dog vendor, our hero listened carefully to his educated son explain the difficult economic conditions around them and that, despite the fact that their business was reaching new levels of success, they must not carelessly trudge forward as if they were unaware of the world around them. Well, knowing his son was much better informed, the father relented and he and his son set about closing locations and discontinued their advertising campaign.

As you might guess, it turns out the educated son's insights could not have been more correct; within months of the closing of locations and the removal of advertising, the hot dog business was no more.

The moral of the story is that it is always easier to be a cynic and give in to whatever force or voice is telling you that you cannot be successful at whatever you may hope to achieve. It is easier to say the market stinks or the economy is bad than to admit you're not saving because it's hard or because you need more self-discipline.

As Nassim Taleb says in his book *The Black Swan,* "Oftentimes what you don't know won't hurt you; conversely, what you incorrectly *think* you know could kill you."

Cynicism is a tool of inaction.

Accept the Chaos, Look for the Opportunity

How is a guy supposed to know dirty clothes go "in" the hamper and not "on" the hamper? How is a guy supposed to know that his wife doesn't know that golf is not just four hours of chasing a little white ball around? The rules of the game very clearly indicate that two hours of post-round drinks and tall tales are part of the deal. Seriously, these things are unknowable to me and my friends, and the list of things we cannot know despite our strong desire "to know" is infinitely long.

What will the market do today, next week, next month, or next year? I DON'T KNOW! What will long-term interest rates be in three years? What will the price of oil be next Tuesday at 3:00 pm? What is the price of tea in China?

Often, clients or potential clients are looking for someone—anyone—to tell them what "is" going to happen in any of the aforementioned instances. They hope that this guy or gal is the one who can tell them when to get in and when to get out.

What do you think the election will do to the markets? I don't know. What do you think China is going to do with all those ghost cities and how does that affect the trade deficit? I DON'T KNOW. Do you think there will be a terrorist attack, and if so, how will it affect the markets? Probably. And…I don't know.

If you ever want out of a political conversation, say the following: "Gosh, that's a complicated issue and I have not studied the facts enough to have a firm opinion either way."

For most of us, this is largely true; of course, it doesn't keep us from an opinion (or our facts). Human beings crave predictability. Unfortunately, the world is largely unpredictable. When natural disasters occur, I am often amazed at the number of people who start pointing fingers and assigning blame. "Clearly, so and so should have seen that tsunami coming and warned us all."

Folks, life and markets are mostly unpredictable, especially in the short term. Understanding and accepting chaos are the keys to success in both. Great investors never panic when something they didn't see coming happens, they merely look for the opportunity in that occurrence. Banking crisis, tech wreck, the Asian Flu, Housing Bubble, 911, Election 2016...holy Moses, almost no one saw any of these things coming.

The danger, my friends, is not in missing the signs of the next great disruption. The danger is believing those who say they do. Those who tell you they can predict the future are one of two things: delusional or manipulative. Neither are good for your life and or wallet.

I see the ex-Treasury Secretary every morning now on TV trying to convince me that I need to buy gold coins because the world is soon gonna stop spinning. On the other channel, some dude is saying I can day-trade my way to riches right after I attend his seminar for $699.00 at the local Marriott. Always keep in mind that where you stand is often largely connected to where you sit. People who get paid to talk...usually do.

Things I do know: hard work, good service, and honesty are things that never go out of style. Your investment professional cannot (with a straight face) tell you exactly where the markets are going, but they *can* return your call promptly, process your paperwork, and conduct transactions quickly. They cannot put you in that one stock that will double this week, but they can thoroughly explain the most efficient way to extract income from your hard-earned savings.

How many times have you said, "If I only knew then, what I know now?"

Well, for starters, the picture of you in the parachute pants and mullet would not be here to amuse us all. Thus, I am for keeping some things a surprise and embracing all that I cannot know.

Look for Someone Who Will Tell You the Truth

My clients allow me to be me. If I'm critical or I push back and say "That's bull," they don't freak out. They don't say, "Can you believe he just said that? I am moving my account!" They get it. I turn a lot of people off, which is fine. It's important we find out if we are compatible right away rather than four years later when the damage is done. Someone wise once said, "Be yourself, it's easier to remember."

But there are people who come here with that *he's going to tell me how to make a million dollars overnight* mentality, that *he's going to earn me 15% a year guaranteed* attitude. But that's not real and I say it's not real; those people leave pretty quickly. Or when I say, "This is my fee," those people say, "Can you do it cheaper?" I say, "Nope." I turn them off. Because if I give YOU a discount, what about the guy who's been my client for 30 years? What am I saying to him?

Health is Wealth

There are a lot of studies, recently collected in *Wheat Belly* by Dr. William Davis, that show an overindulgence in wheat, in sugar, in processed foods, and in meat, to a certain extent, has neurological effects and can worsen anxiety. People can't think clearly, they're lethargic. People are literally shuffling around like zombies. You can't shuffle around, and be uncomfortable, and be unhappy, and be self-conscious, and be on seven different drugs AND concentrate on your money. You can't! You're too distracted.

We've all been sick, right? You don't want to talk to anyone! You don't want to do anything! *I feel like crap! I don't want to talk about THAT.* The more you feel poorly, the less likely it is that you'll be able to focus on the tasks that will get you from Point A to Point B.

Health is everything. Health is where it all starts, yet the medical community prescribes drugs to keep you chronically ill. It's not an intentional conspiracy, but that *is* what they're doing. If you walk into your doctor and say, "I have high cholesterol," she's not going to say, "Stop doing this, get on a treadmill, work out." She'll say, "Here's some Lipitor." Unfortunately, the Lipitor masks the problem; it doesn't fix it.

I understood early on in life what sugar does to you. My father is a diabetic, so I totally understand the effects. And sometimes, it's unavoidable. It's bad luck. My dad was skinny as a rail, he just inherited it from his parents. Knock on wood, so far, I've been lucky. But I've also been very aware of it. I'm fighting it. I wake up every day and work hard to not get diabetes.

The economic implications of an ultra-processed diet are immense. From Medicare to Medicaid to GDP, you could go on forever about what that means, but I will not be quiet about it. Health is the key to life. Money without health is pointless. I mentor many young people, and I refuse to accept poor health due to ignorance.

Key Chapter 5 Takeaways:

- Don't thrash around. Find the rhythm of saving, spending, and investing.
- Worry only about what you can actually control.
- Accept chaos and change.
- Try to relax.
- Sleep on it.
- Work with an advisor who will tell you the truth, and be willing to pay for that expertise.
- Don't let gloom and doom thinking take over.
- Health is wealth. Stop eating so much sugar.

I've Never Made Anyone Rich

Chapter 6
The Media and the "Experts"

> *Rather than love, than money, than fame, give me truth.*
> *~Henry David Thoreau*

Let's face it: "If it bleeds, it leads." The media over-hypes violence and crime, even though this is, statistically, the safest time to have ever been alive. If you watch the news all day long—first of all GET A LIFE—second of all, you will become convinced that the world is indeed about to end.

"News" organizations are in the business of selling advertising. Nobody gives a crap how nice of a day YOU had! If someone got carjacked in Peoria, then, by god, you're gonna hear about it, not once but over and over again. Again, "Plane Lands Safely" is never gonna sell ad space, and they (the media) know it.

That's the same media, whether it's *Money Magazine* or the financial media or the *Wall Street Journal,* telling readers and viewers all of the people in financial services are out to steal from them. If they put out a headline that reads "It's important to save and no amount of fees shopping and or stock picking will ever change that," NOBODY will read that article. If they put out a headline that says, "Ten ways your advisor is ripping you off, and why investment people eat babies," that's the one you're gonna read; you know you would.

The Experts

In matters of the heart, not unlike matters of the wallet, "expert" is always a moniker we attach with great trepidation. Or it should be.

There are so many clever names for market trends these days. You got the Flash Crash, The Tech Wreck, The Asian Contagion, and the always popular Triple Witch Hitch. Sounds like the lineup to a WWF event. "SUNDAY, SUNDAY, SUNDAY! See the ultimate showdown between The Asian Contagion and The Tech Wreck! Gates open at noon!"

As I get to coffee number two this morning, I've seen no less than three different "experts" proclaim with extreme confidence and the usual amount of ambiguity that the markets will behave one way or another. The problem is they all ooze confidence as they each say something different. At 7:00, I was convinced the run would continue to 45,000 on the Dow only to be told at 7:15 that we could be in for a ten percent decline by the end of March.

Luckily, the tiebreaker came on at 7:30, and with the utmost certainty, this soothsayer explained there would be lots of volatility this year and to, I quote, "ACT ACCORDINGLY." WHAT!? *Act accordingly.* What in the hell does *that* mean? I always act accordingly. If it's raining, I act accordingly and get an umbrella. If I hit a bad golf shot, I throw my seven iron into a nearby pond, which in my book is "acting accordingly."

What in the world are we all supposed to glean from three corporate types in $1,000 suits telling us essentially nothing? I'll tell you what: NOTHING. As I have pointed out to you many times throughout this book, an expert is someone who knows just a bit more than you do on a subject, and more often than not wants to sell you something.

These clowns all come with the appropriate levels of alphabet soup next to their names and come from the best firms. Unfortunately, so did Bernie Madoff and the guys who ran Lehman Brothers off a cliff. In the end, saving, investing, and appreciating money is no different than romance. One must trust their instincts and work hard at their relationships to have success in either.

Eliminate the Smoke and Mirrors

The layer of costs associated with investing that can be eliminated include the research and the management—a lot of that can go away. The reason it can go away is markets are efficient. Trying to outsmart markets has never, ever, ever worked. Never. It works for a period of time until it doesn't. There's a guy named Bill Miller who worked for Legg Mason. He's a legend who got his ass kicked for many years in a row starting in 2007. He beat the market every year... except for the years when he didn't; his Value Fund lost more than half its value as Miller held onto bets on Bear Sterns and AIG long after others split. So, that's not beating the market every year, now, is it?

They're selling this idea: "If you come to Chase, or you come to Goldman Sachs, we have the secrets!" They each say it, but they can't all be right, can they?

We can get rid of the analytics that don't work; a lot of the green and red blinking lights that people seem to be attracted to on the trading platforms are meaningless. We can get rid of the day traders and the penny stocks, and all the stuff that never works for long. We can get rid of all of that, and just have people buy quality companies on the cheapest platform, and get advice from human advisors on taxes, estate planning, Social Security benefits,

Medicare processing, the list goes on and on and on. This is the part of the process that's meaningful, and that helps people.

The rest of the analysis that Wall Street and the media is selling is just smoke and mirrors.

Research Analysts

It's a marketing tool. They say, "We have these great analysts!" There are not many analysts I would give a plug nickel for. The thing about these market strategists and analytical people is that they're never wrong, according to them. They're just off because of *this*—they always have an explanation for why they're wrong. "Well, I said the S&P 500 was going to be up 30%, and it's only up five. I was right, except the government did *this*, or some geopolitical issue occurred, or there was a catastrophe in California and the mudslide caused oranges to not be shipped this month." So, they weren't *wrong*. They were right, except they were completely wrong.

That goes on constantly. I've called out my own firm for stock information, called the analysts, and said, "You cover XYZ, what can you tell me about earnings and/or any other meaningful data?" The reply is always, "Well, I have to look it up." What do you mean you have to look it up? I thought you covered this company and knew the stock inside and out?! But they don't. A lot of them are 25 years old, they don't know…they have no better understanding than you do.

Often, a client who works at a company, let's pretend it's Boeing, will ask, "What do you think about Boeing?" I'll say, "I think they make airplanes. You know way more about Boeing than I do. Why could I possibly tell *you* about a place you're at each day?" People often say, "What is this stock going to do?" I say, "It'll pay a dividend and go up over the next twenty years, probably."

The things that drive monumental shifts in a stock cannot be known. Lumber Liquidators is a good example. The stock dropped from $40 or $50 down to $10 or something because they realized that the lumber was filled with formaldehyde and was coming from China. I could've read a thousand spreadsheets, yet there was no way for me to know this revelation was going to happen. People would say, "Why didn't you know that?" *Because that is not knowable.* How am I supposed to know if the CEO is having an affair with the CFO? I don't know!

This idea that these research firms or media analysts know the gyrations of the market is wrong. Nobody got up on September 11 at 8:00 a.m. and said, "I think the market's going to drop 3,000 points." Nobody had that conversation.

Ninety percent of a stock's movement, give or take a couple of percentage points depending on who you ask, is based on the market. So, if it's a shitty stock, and the market's up 400 points tomorrow, that shitty stock's probably going to be up.
If it's the "greatest stock ever," if it's Amazon, and they've put every retailer in this country out of business yet the market drops 2,000 points tomorrow, Amazon's is most likely going to go down.

Still, people emphasize the 10% they can't control rather than the 90% they can.

They can control time. They can say, "I'm going to buy IBM, Microsoft, Apple, Johnson & Johnson, and Procter & Gamble, and I'm going to hold them for the next 30 years. I don't care what happens, we need ketchup, we need toothpaste, we need computers," and know that's probably going to work and cost next to nothing.

Index Funds: The Media Darling

"How does that compare to the S&P 500 over the last few years?" If I had a dollar for every time I heard this over the last twenty-four months, to quote the Barenaked Ladies, "I'd be rich!"

For those of you not keeping score at home, the S&P 500 is an unmanaged index of stocks used by media and the like as a kind of de facto scorecard for the overall return of the stock market. In fact, many folks consider it the end all, be all in investing and measuring their own portfolios—that is, when it's going up. In 2008, nobody called me up and asked if their returns were in line with the S&P 500. Why? Oh, I think you know why: the S&P 500 was down 37% and, of course, NO ONE wants to be down 37%.

So why now, why all the interest in comparing themselves to the S&P 500? Well for one, the media has been using this as the one and only way to measure investment performance for the better part of 50 years. They have *trained* you to think this way. Yes, you! The person who can't be fooled by "the media!"

But Scott, you say, "How else should we measure our success or lack thereof?" Well, I'm glad you asked. Success, like many things, deserves thoughtful context. Should I assume I am a slow runner because I cannot run as fast as Usain Bolt, or that my golf game is shameful (okay, on some days it is) because I don't stand a chance against Dustin Johnson? The answer is maybe. But what if my goals are *not* to run as fast as Mr. Bolt or to hit a golf ball as far as Mr. Johnson? What if my goals are to run well for my age and beat a dollar or two each weekend out of the other hacks I spend my Saturdays with?

What if your goals are to retire in X amount of years with Y amount of money coming into your household and not to "beat" some arbitrary index? By the way, did you know there are over 100 indexes that can be tracked or used to measure investment performance? Bond indexes, stock indexes, hybrid indexes, commodity indexes, fat kids, skinny kids, even kids with Chicken Pox! Remember that? Armour hot dogs aside, it's time to forget the indexes and instead develop your own goals, not to use those set forth by the investment industry that you will likely never achieve.

How 'bout we save enough and act responsibly enough to get where we are going no matter what the index du jour does? While I am not predicting this, it is entirely possible the S&P 500 will be at the same level it is today ten years from now. Then what? You've counted on a return that you are not only not guaranteed to get, but likely will not get 'cause life is just that way. Sure, knowing how your basket of stuff compares to a benchmark basket of stuff can be helpful, but maybe your hopes and dreams should not be pinned to an arbitrary basket of anything, but on years of thoughtful planning and saving.

I Almost Never Fall into a Sinkhole

In his recent article "Why We Love Bad News," Ray Williams (creator of "Wired for Success") notes we are hardwired to react to, and in fact gravitate toward, bad news. Moreover, thousands of years ago, it was not only understandable that we took note of bad news, but imperative that we noted it and spread it. If a guy walks into your cave and mentions he saw a saber-toothed tiger, I'm thinking alarms need to be going off in your brain and your neighbors are gonna be quite annoyed if you keep that to yourself.

Our minds are far more stimulated chemically by bad news than good news. This is so well known to the media outlets and their battalion of psychologists that some estimates have us watching as many as 17 negative reports for every positive one. The truth is that bad stuff happens (no revelation there), but by and large, it does not happen to you very often.

In a city of a million plus, at least once a day someone has something bad happen to them. Of course, the other 999,999 of us generally don't get attacked and I almost never fall into a sinkhole. To that end, since 1973 FBI statistics show that in 2009 aggravated assaults were down to 320 per year for every 100,000 persons versus 1973, in which the number was 1250 per 100,000 persons. Violent crime overall has dropped over that same time frame from 4770 events per 100,000 persons to a 2009 number of 1690 per person. I realize this might seem counterintuitive to most of you, especially if you are a news junkie. For the record, I have not watched the "news" in about 20 years.

It seems that way largely because the media is so adept at bombarding us with negative messages that you, like Chicken Little, have become convinced the sky is constantly falling. If one idiot shoots another anywhere in town, you get to hear about it for weeks if not months.

My point? As Flavor Flav of the groundbreaking hip-hop band Public Enemy once said, "Don't believe the hype."

Every day in our little community, people are living wonderful lives and raising awesome children in a largely safe and prosperous community. For sure, in all of our lives a little rain must and will fall, but if you spend all your time in a rain suit and mukluks, the guys with butterfly nets and white suits will eventually come for you.

To be successful in saving and investing, you must have a very strong filter for bad news. In 2008, the world was indeed ending for many of you. Every day, you were bombarded by negative messages that, at least on the surface, made you feel like ammunition and corn seed were your only options. Of course, today we know this was indeed hype.

I tell you this because it's likely to happen again. Maybe today, maybe three years from now. We will go through tough times and folks will tell you, "It's different this time." It may be different this time, but the outcome will likely be the same. The courageous and disciplined will stay the course and reap the benefits; the majority will stay glued to the television and fall further behind. 'Till then, keep smiling and enjoy your uneventful day.

Let's Talk Mutual Friends—Because I May NOT Discuss Actual Investment Products Candidly

There's a reason financial media is terrible. Let's look at that reason.

Based on a recent regulation that has since been reversed, there was a significant span of time in which I could describe any actual investment products in my column. As you will recall, back in 2008 or so, the world nearly fell apart due to the selfish and irresponsible actions of a handful of major players on Wall Street. These greedy SOBs created a frothy market of mortgage-backed securities (see *The Big Short*) that generated billions in fees without any regard for their validity or potential liability to the American taxpayer.

In addition to the firms that created the mess, the ratings agencies (you know their names) joined in the party by rating the junk they were selling as investment grade right up until the moment they fell apart. Why, you ask? Because they got paid to do so and who's gonna call out the goose who is laying the golden eggs?

In the end, we all know who paid...we did.

Literally ONE guy went to jail and he was some mid-level sacrificial lamb the firms offered up. Not only did we pay in terms of the deficit we are now saddled with, but we paid in the losses in our 401(k)s and our brokerage accounts.

What came from that was a regulatory firestorm of politicians trying to squash any potential for this to happen again. Of course, when something is broken, it makes sense we should try to fix it. So, fix it, they did. A slew of new regulations came to be and they let the rotten sons of guns have it. That's right, they let financial advisors who had nothing to do with it have it with both barrels.

They decided not to pursue the executives of these major firms, but instead create important rules that prevent a guy like me from saying the actual name of any investment product in a book like this. Now, to be fair, under that regulation, I could say those words if I paid the toll. I could have submitted my writing to the governing authorities, and in return for a nominal fee, they would review my offering. To be clear...I REFUSED.

I would imagine that if you read enough investment-related periodicals you might say, "but Scott, I read about investment products and their uses all of the time in magazines and the like."

True, but those things are written by 26-year-old journalists (not that there's anything wrong with that) and nothing stops them from having strong opinions as they are not licensed with government agencies. Oh, the irony.

You're Not Going to Find a Secret in the Media

Mostly because there are no secrets. You want to become more informed? More financially savvy? Go to the people who are successful. Read a book by Warren Buffett. Read a book by Tim Ferriss. Tony Robbins.

The funny thing about the Richard Bransons and the Mark Cubans of the world? They can't wait to tell you. They want desperately to tell you how they succeeded. The problem is, 98 out of 100 people who read Bill Gates or Tim Ferriss won't act on it, or they'll think they can't do it. They think there's something special about these individuals. There *is* something special, but nothing that you don't possess. The big names were just able to bring it out and act on it.

Read *The Millionaire Next Door*. That is the book to read. That is the pinnacle of everything. It's simply about living beneath your means, which is so un-American. Sure, sometimes it's fun to be an American! But if you don't see it for what it is, it will devour you.

I don't dislike the media; I'm not a "fake news" guy. I just think journalism has gotten so spread out, there are so many sources for it now, and it's gotten watered down and lazy, for the most part. I read the same article a hundred times. It's lacking any detail or thoughtfulness, especially about this industry: "Fees are too high! Learn how to reduce your fees! Your returns are too low, learn how to increase your returns!" It's all crap. The headline is, "Top 15 Funds This Year, Top 7 Stocks That'll Improve Your Wealth!" It's all lists, Americans love their lists. Give me something meaningful.

Key Chapter 6 Takeaways:

- The media wants to keep you agitated.
- If you want to become successful or more financially savvy, go right to the experts themselves. They're dying to tell you everything they know.
- There are no "secrets" in the media.
- One reason the media has bad information is because advisors have to deal with silly regulations about what they can and cannot talk about.
- Be skeptical of advertising in a bull market.
- Be careful about who you consider to be an expert.

Chapter 7
Reflections on 37 Years in the Business

He who rejects change is the architect of decay. The only human institution which rejects progress is the cemetery.
~Harold Wilson

I got into this business because I was infatuated with markets, not that I had any technical expertise—in fact, I had very little technical expertise or understanding of it, yet I was always interested in it. I didn't know what it meant; I thought I was going to go be an analyst and study stocks, and make great recommendations to people about what stocks they could buy, and cultivate some brilliance on markets. I quickly realized that when you get into the brokerage business, you're a salesperson. That was the bad news. The good news, I was good at it. I'm persistent. I'm fairly disciplined and thick headed, so "no" doesn't mean a whole lot to me. Which was good, because I got told no a lot.

I think most people get into this business because they see it as a shortcut—there's that word again—to wealth, without being a doctor or a lawyer or something like that. The truth of the matter is, for every 100 people who try to do this, 99 of them fail. I've probably seen a thousand people come and go in this business who couldn't cut it. It's a hard business; it's immensely harder than you think, because people will tell you to get lost. People don't want to give you their money. They want to tell you to go away, especially when you're young. I, quite frankly, don't know why anybody gave me money the first ten years of my career. I'm thankful they did, but I don't know why they did.

If you can survive, there *is* money in this business, though there's less easy money in it than there used to be. It used to be pretty simple to make at least a decent amount of money without much effort. I don't think that's as true as it used to be. They're requiring more of advisors these days; we have to have a higher level of skill. That's been brought on by legislation, and the public requires more of their advisors than they used to. It used to be, the advisor sold you a mutual fund when you had money, and didn't talk to you again for three years when you didn't. If the thing they sold you worked, you gave them more of your money, and if it didn't, you went somewhere else. That's kind of how the business functioned, and that's why advisors used to constantly be on the hunt for new clients.

Advisors do two things. They manage money, and they sell stuff. One of those activities pays them. Which one do you think they're doing the most of? Fortunately, those ideas are no longer unaffiliated. They came back together with fee-based planning, which has been a great revelation. Things have changed for the better, and advisors are held more accountable. People are more aware of what they're paying, which is a good thing. But the general public lacks perspective—fees have been compressed by two-thirds since I've been in the business. People know *what* they're paying yet they don't really know *why*.

Another change is firms are offering better tools for planning. We have some amazing software now that really is helpful and impactful for the client. Having said that, I still think it's the minority of advisors who really care about outcomes. Most of the insurance agents, the captive agents that work selling annuities all the time, and even some of the large firm guys and people like that, they're just trying to do a trade. Most of the time.

The Certified Financial Planner™ (CFP™) Designation

I believe it is overrated, but I don't mean that it's not hard to achieve. It's a hard test; there's a lot of studying. I have CFPs™ here at my practice, but I don't judge them by an accreditation or an acronym. I refuse. Because they're trying to make it the standard, which is an exclusionary practice. CFP™ was something they just *gave* you fifteen years ago if you'd been in the business long enough, but it then became a barrier to entry. What I mean by that is, some financial advisors likely began to collude and say, "Well, now we're going to make it hard, because we don't want you taking our money from us."

The truth of the matter is the CFP™ is a great curriculum, it's helpful to some degree. But most, in my opinion, of what those pursuing the acronym learn they don't use, because a lot of it is not associated with the day-to-day of what we do. Yet they're trying to make it the standard, and they hold themselves out as some "holier-than-thou" organization. But if you look at arbitration cases, more than a few of them involve CFPs™. I believe just because you have an acronym at the end of your name, does not make you trustworthy or honorable, nor does it even make you smart. It just means you took a test.

I'm not diminishing the effort it takes to get it. It is a hard test and a tough curriculum. But it has, often, zero impact on client outcomes. What it does show is someone's willingness to put that effort in, which is not nothing.

The Series 7 test is also hard. But again, it just shows a general understanding of the curriculum in a certain academic capacity. There's no test that says you're going to work hard, be honorable, or provide good outcomes. That test doesn't exist.

I think we place, as a society, way too much emphasis on these acronyms that, really, are about the fees those acronyms generate. Because not only does the CFP™ designation cost several thousand dollars to get, you have to re-up every year; you have to do continuing education. Let's face it, it's a business. It's not worthless, but it's not the only thing to consider.

It's not to say you shouldn't work with someone who is a CFP™. All I'm saying is, it's not the end all, be all that they'd like to make you believe it is.

I have all the acronyms and licenses you're supposed to have. Trust me, the continuing ed, in my opinion, is worthless. You have to go to conferences, or go to a lunch or a dinner, or do it online. It's all a money grab.

Eric Hoffer explains it perfectly: "Every great cause begins as a movement, becomes a business and eventually degenerates into a racket." See: unions, charities, countries, fraternal and business organizations. The CFP™ was a cause that became a business and is desperately trying to become a racket. The same is true of the SEC and most other regulatory bodies.

Build a Process

My man John Cougar Mellencamp (or is it just John Mellencamp these days? When you find him, let me know) had a song out years ago called "Stand for Something." In the chorus, he pointed out (quite emphatically, I might add) that if you "don't stand right up for something, you're gonna fall...for anything" followed by those unforgettable lyrics, "yeah, yeah, yeah...yeah, yeah, yeah."

Nearly 30 years removed from that soaking wet "Rock Super Bowl" these words still ring true.

Many investors have unwittingly gotten into the habit of forgoing the arduous task of developing a process for their investable dollars. They wander from investment to investment and sometimes broker to broker in search of the next great idea.

The bad news is that everyone they meet…has one. Why, history is filled with great idea men who were more than willing to share their brilliance with those seeking an easy path to financial freedom. Their names include Ponzi, Milken, Boesky and, most recently, Madoff. I am absolutely astounded that CNBC can fill a month's worth of 10 pm slots with *American Greed* episodes. Night after night, I watch (to my wife's annoyance) as idea man after idea man steals not hundreds, not thousands, but millions of dollars from those hooked on the notion that a miracle is right around the corner if you just look hard enough.

As the saying goes, ideas are not just a dime a dozen; often they are *a lifetime of savings* a dozen.

If you walk into a financial services company asking for their hottest idea, odds are that's what they will sell you—yesterday's hot idea! Investment management companies are really good at printing nice shiny brochures with last year's or the last few years' returns on them for your edification. The good news for most money managers is that they have sometimes dozens of funds, and while many will not do well in a given year, they have the luxury of cherry picking the ones that do and selling them to the brokerage industry to be sold to you.

To avoid such pitfalls, one need only take a little time to build a process. Obvious questions that should be now percolating in your head include "what is a process? and "how do I get one?" An investment process is really a matter of setting disciplines for one's self. It could be as simple as adding $100.00 to the market every month that ends with a negative return, or deeply complex like those used by large endowments such as Harvard and Yale.

Do you really think the folks at Princeton are waiting for a hot tip from their cousin Louie who "has really changed since his three-to-five-year vacation?" I think not. At these institutions, they have rigid disciplines for how and when they will invest. The Dow goes down, they do "A;" interest rates go up, they do "B." Yours need not be as complex as the bookworms in the Ivy League (no offense to smart people), but a process, no matter the complexities, is a worthwhile endeavor.

Whether we are talking exercise, academics or investing, discipline is the key to success. It will not always make you right and it will not always make you money, but it will keep you from falling for anything...yeah, yeah, yeah.

Beware Unintended Consequences

First of all, I'm not a political person; let's get that out of the way. I'm in the "you be nice to me and I'll be nice to you" camp. Truthfully, unless you are running for office or intend to start a revolution, your noisy self-righteous blather is just that.

Now that I have sufficiently ticked off both sides of the aisle, let's get down to business. Over the last few months, I have found myself in the crosshairs of numerous regulators. Let me tell you, there are a lot of regulators, and that makes for the "Don King" of crosshairs. (If you're under 40, Google it.)

So, as you can see, it is basically the full-time job, now, of small business people to fill out forms and answer ridiculous questionnaires in order to appease the many federal, state, county and city regulators that are literally competing with each other to regulate/fine small businesspeople. Before you go assigning me some sort of anti-government political label, understand I realize regulation is important and should exist to protect us all from the rotten eggs amongst us.

What I take issue with is the notion of "shoot first, ask questions later." One of those aforementioned departments spent four hours in my office grilling my partner about a $58.00 issue. That's right, they spent hundreds of taxpayer dollars and many hours of my partner's and my time trying to get to the bottom of a $58.00 issue. I guess what I want politicians and citizens alike to recognize is that more rules and more departments are not the answer to white collar crime, or any other crime for that matter. More questions like, "Have you ever committed a felony or been accused of committing a felony?" are pointless.

NEWS FLASH #1: the bad guys are also going to say no to that question. Bad guys do not fill out questionnaires honestly; the only ones you are snaring in these ridiculous nets are the good guys. I can already see the next wave of inquiry: "Mr. Brown, is it true you have not been diligently keeping up with your customers' accounts?" "Yes, because I spend all day answering stupid questions, an impediment to success criminals do not have!"

The political answer to all problems is more rules. Listen up! More rules only do one thing: slow business and add to regulatory payrolls. Every year, the prospectuses we are mandated to hand out get thicker and thicker.

NEWS FLASH #2: NOBODY READS THEM. Raise your hand if you have *ever* read a prospectus. Okay, now lower your hand if you're an SEC attorney. Now lower your hand if you're an engineer (I know about you guys). Okay, that leaves about two out of one hundred. The most hilarious thing about disclaimers and "sign here" documentation is that if you don't sign it, you ain't getting whatever product or service you seek to attain.

Do you really think it matters what the Apple disclaimer says? "Um yes, could I speak to Tim Cook?" Tim: "Oh hello, Scott. I'm so glad you called." Me: "Yeah Tim, I looked over iTunes' agreement and I have a problem with line seven on page three. Could you guys amend that for me? Then I think I'm good to go on Madonna's Greatest hits." (Don't judge, you know you like "Papa Don't Preach.")

Tim: "Scott I hear you on line seven; unfortunately, we sell millions of songs each day to people who check a box on an agreement they did not read, but lawyers say we have to have it in case the lawyers from any number of regulators come calling. So, in short, pound sand." Me: "Okay thanks, Tim, and good luck with that $500 Timex you're selling."

In the end, it's all an effort to legislate honesty. Again, not gonna happen. I would say most businesspeople are honest and well-intended. More rules simply lead to more work and more shortcuts being taken by normally well-intended people. More rules also lead to more staff (ask your doctor about this one...and stand back), and more staff leads to more cost which leads to higher prices.

Liberal Dreamers vs. Conservative Realists

Politics, politics, politics...to me, it's such a pointless conversation. People believe what they believe and nobody's ever going to change. Nobody's interested in your point of view. Go cast your vote and then get on with your life, because if you spend all day watching whatever your flavor of news is, and let it affect your investment decisions, that's unwise. We know, statistically, that there is very little separation between Democrats and Republicans when it comes to returns.

The only byproduct of politics that frustrates me is it frightens people. I get tired of telling others the world isn't going to end. And that even if it *is* going to end because the politician you didn't like won...there's literally no place you can put your money that is going to be unaffected. So again, the politics are problematic only in how they affect decision-making.

Like anybody else, I have political sensibilities, although less and less these days. And like anybody else, I have my worries about the way policies are enacted and things are run but it doesn't play into my decision making at all. I don't say, "I'm not buying this stock because so and so is running," or "I'm not going to invest in bonds because this senator won." No. At the end of the day, I make the decisions the same way, Democrat or Republican.

I'm accused by my friends of being a liberal, which is hilarious. Being pinned down as one or the other is just childish, it's a shortcut to call someone a name. Some people attach themselves to those names proudly, which I think is foolish because now you're just reading from a checklist: well, I'm a liberal so I believe these things, or I'm a conservative, so I believe these things. What if you believe some of each? Is that possible?

I am an issue person. If you want to talk to me about economics, I'm probably more fiscally conservative. I believe in hard work, I believe that giving people things isn't always a great idea, not only for you, but for them.

At the same time, I don't love some of the social agenda on the conservative side, and the narrow-mindedness of it; what I perceive to be thoughtlessness on certain issues. I guess that's where my liberal tag comes from. The problem is, there is no middle anymore. The extremes are the only sides, and they refuse, out of principle, to see things the same way as someone across the aisle.

There's a practicality on the conservative side that I appreciate, and I also like the heart side of it. It used to be, that in the middle were people who could talk and work out a solution. Now, they're not allowed. So, we get what we have, which is complete gridlock.

Beware the Wolves

If you are like me (old) you grew up watching the cartoon series *Looney Tunes*. I am sure none of you are surprised by this revelation. One of my favorite segments was the "Sheepdog and the Wolf," or the Sheepdog and what appears to be Wile E. Coyote's brother Ralph. As most of you know, Sheepdog Sam spends his days watching over the flock and protecting them from the ever-present danger of Ralph, the antihero. Of course, in any given episode Sam spends a great deal of time pounding our poor incompetent hunter Ralph into submission as he fruitlessly tries to grab some lamb chops for the night's feast.

The part that I always loved, and still reference today, especially when discussing politics, is the point at the end of each day when the two characters, despite their antagonistic relationship, meet at the time clock to punch out and exchange pleasantries. "Alright Sam, great day...see you tomorrow." "Thanks, Ralph. Have a nice night."

I get the impression our politicians do much of the same. Each day they tear each other apart in an attempt to garner votes and please whatever group they covet that day, and then meet at the local bar to discuss the score of the basketball game.

I would bet, to the buying public, the investment business has to feel much the same. If you have more than a buck or two, everyone on Wall Street wants it. The advisor down the street, the insurance agent, the banker, the mortgage broker, the real estate agent and the pastor all want a share of your dough. I have to think this is not only confusing, but might be downright terrifying. In this scenario, *you* are the sheep. It's not all bad being a sheep unless you struggle to tell the difference between the wolf and the sheepdog.

In my business, and I dare say in some of the others I mentioned, there are sheepdogs and there are wolves. They sound the same, they look the same, and the sheep cannot tell them apart. The sad part is that often the wolf gets the business from you because his or her story is usually better than the sheepdog's. The sheepdog will often say things like, "I have a process that is not perfect, but will, I believe, with discipline and perseverance get you where you want to go." Conversely, the wolf will say, "Oh my gosh! You are in that!? I would have never put you in that! All of my clients earned X percentage last year."

The formula for X is whatever you earned plus some additional amount, but not enough to raise suspicion (we call that the Madoff formula). The sheepdog might say, "Let's build the most conservative portfolio we can that also allows you the opportunity to help make a competitive return, knowing we will have good years and bad years."

The wolf would say, "I know exactly where this market is going and I'd bet my new Ferrari I can get you 12% per year." The sheepdog would say, "I can't promise you anything other than hard work, honesty and a commitment by me, my staff, and our affiliates to provide you a top notch experience no matter what the markets bring."

In the end, many a sheep ends up on the menu at the wolf's shop with no way to know until it's too late. In each of the financial professions I have mentioned, there are both sheepdogs and wolves. I promise your little community has a good amount of the former; just be careful to make sure the one you choose is standing guard, not preparing the gravy.

It's especially hard to spot the wolves when you're asking for a wolf. I think a lot of times people get exactly what they're asking for. I've had people walk in here and say, "I'm shopping around for an advisor. The last guy said he's got this super awesome process and he can probably earn me 12%, 15% a year." My response to that is to simply say, "You should probably go with him. I'm not guaranteeing you anything; markets provide what they provide. You plant a bunch of orange trees and it doesn't rain for six months, you're probably not going to get many oranges. But if they're there to pick, I'll get them."

A lot of people want to know, "What did you earn last year?" The trouble is, the wolf is most likely not going to show you a negative return. He'll likely show you one of his 80 accounts that did pretty well. You get what you ask for.

- If you walk into an advisor's office and they have a solution before you've shared the problem, that's a warning sign.
- If you walk in and they agree with everything you say, that's a warning sign. This is not a person who wants to *grow* your money, they just *want* your money.

Reflecting on the Florida Real Estate Model

The Florida model goes like this: we're going to build you the biggest house on the smallest lot that we can put you in, and we're going to find financing that allows you to make your payment and not much else. The problem with that is, I bet if you dropped me in any subdivision in Florida, short of Isleworth or somewhere where the barrier to entry is a million plus, I could probably tell you how old it is. Based on the number of rentals, based on graffiti, the disrepair...

My wife's mom lives in a place called Buena Ventura Lakes. When they moved there, it was this shining community on a hill, a place where a middle-class family could get a really nice house. They wedged these families into these homes they could barely afford—but they *could* afford—quote unquote...but the families couldn't afford to keep the yards up. They couldn't afford to fix it if something fell apart. Over time, people just gave up. Eventually, those neighborhoods imploded on themselves. They became a high percentage of rentals, and then the whole thing just cascades downward. You don't have owners anymore, people have fled because the neighborhood started to go downhill—and then the neighborhood *really* went downhill. Because you have a bunch of people who don't care, they're parking their cars on the yard. It's just a disaster waiting to happen.

I've Never Made Anyone Rich

Deltona is a great example. Thirty years ago, Deltona, Florida was an immaculate place. The story was, sell your place in New Jersey for $600k, buy one here for $200k, and life will be wonderful...except it's not. Deltona looks like a bomb went off in it. And I can tell you, this will happen here again. It's just a matter of time, unless it's a super high-end community.

We have a *design* here in Florida. We attract you—to this shiny, sunny, stucco, tiled, bathtub-sized swimming pool facility—and we make sure you've got $4,000 a month in income. You're only spending $2,800 on your house, giving you $1,200 to live the rest of your life. There's no room for maintenance; there's no room for the lawn mower. The bomb will go off again. It goes off every ten, fifteen, twenty years. People have already forgotten about 2008/2009.

The people who are millionaires have lived in the same house for the last 30 years. They didn't succumb to the standard line: "Now, you're a freshly married couple, so of course an 1,800 square foot house makes sense. But now you have a baby, so you need to upgrade to 3,000, and it needs to be fancy. Oh! Well, you've got three kids? You've got to have 5,000 square feet now!" People just keep doing this, and they never catch up. Now they're 63, and they probably still have ten years left on their mortgage, and their house probably isn't worth nearly what they paid for it.

I've heard people say, "Well, the wife's pregnant, so I guess we're going to get a bigger house." I always reply with that old joke, "Dude, I've seen your wife. She's not THAT big. She'll still fit in the house you have."

In the 1950s, the average family of four lived in a house that was 1500 square feet. Now we've got bonus rooms measuring 1,500 square feet that, by the way, nobody's going in. So, it's...consume,

consume, consume. Many millennials and Gen X people saw their parents fall apart in 2008, and that's why a lot of them don't want to buy homes now. Which, I think, is an overreaction to the first overreaction. You've got to live somewhere, so why are you paying someone else's mortgage?

The Truth from an Insider

Why is it we love the idea of "insider information?" It kills me when someone tries to tell me they have heard the "scoop" on a company or industry and would like to trade on it. In the 1920s, possibly through the 1980s, there was a decent chance that you might have heard or read something about a company that had not been disseminated and distributed to the masses.

As the 90s wore on, this possibility largely evaporated. Now trading advantages supposedly held by the super-studious researching types and so called "experts" (defined as someone who knows just a bit more than you do) have all but vanished. Today, information of all kinds is available to all of us in the amount of time it takes to type GO. (Yeah, you only need to type GO to get to a Google search. I mean who has two seconds to type the whole word?)

Anyway, any information you think you have on the sly falls into one of two categories: Category A: *Seriously, we all knew that two days ago* and B: Insider information. *Please turn to the right, what size orange jumper do you wear?*

This brings me to what I really mean by insider information. Last week, I returned home from a 10 day adventure with 50 or so of my fellow advisors. Someday when my nausea subsides, ask me about the boat trip across the North Atlantic. Twenty-foot seas aside, I wanted to share with you, the viewing public, my impressions of the financial services industry from the inside. Before I do, please realize that most, in fact, all of these folks come from somewhere other than Wall Street. They came from places like Iowa, Colorado, Texas and, yes, Florida. These advisors were not your run-of-the-mill annuity salesman. They were, in fact, the cream of the crop and cumulatively responsible for north of $20 billion in client assets. On average, they had over 20 years of experience and numerous academic credentials.

What I learned about them and shared with our little team over on Rugby Street is the following:

> 1. They are kind, giving people. It floors me that the most generous and thoughtful advisors are also the most financially successful. Call it karma or Universal Balance, but these people very much care about others. After countless industry shindigs, the lesson I keep learning about the advisory community is that the more successful the advisor, the more likely they are to be a good person.

> 2. They are big picture people. None of them talk about outsmarting the market or the time they bought Apple and it doubled. They talk about clients and client success. They talk about the client's daughter who went to college and medical school because they bugged the father when she was two to start saving. Likely that father never "beat" the market, but because that advisor pestered him, his daughter is now saving lives in Denver. They talk about the postcard from Europe that their 30-year client sent them describing the first post-retirement trip they had taken.

None of these advisors promise to beat the market because none of them can. A good financial advisor earns their fee not by beating or keeping up with any ridiculous benchmark (they have index funds for nearly free if that is your need.) They earn their keep by answering the phone when you are nervous, and by helping you decide between ROTH and Traditional IRAs. They earn their fee by running the calculations on what you're saving, your goals, and the likelihood of success.

They earn their fee by telling you when you aren't doing what you need to be successful. They tell you the doggone truth, NOT WHAT YOU WANT TO HEAR! What you often want to hear is that there are shortcuts and that they (the advisor) will earn you a return that is superior to the guy down the street. I, and other great advisors, will not do that. The things I would look for in my advisor are experience, honesty, responsive service, and an understandable process. To a person, these top people provide that. Sure, good returns help, but they are not to be counted on. If it's the basis for your relationship, it is likely unhealthy for both of you.

In the end, if you're looking for an advisor or considering a change, for me the criteria is simple. Are they responsive and do they care? If so, keep 'em. They are rare.

Wall Street and the Individual Investor

Wall Street consists of the entrenched corporate financial entities that control three quarters of the world's money supply. These entities are interested in getting Americans to buy products, whether those products are research, mutual funds, managers of some type, annuities, insurance, derivatives like from '07 and '08, bonds, whatever it is they're selling. A group of major players—you know the names—those large corporations are quietly, and sometimes not so quietly, trying to convince the public to look away from themselves and toward myself and my colleagues: "Don't look at us! Look at these advisors ripping you off!"

They're not blatantly saying it, because advisors generate a lot of revenue for them, but they are slowly trying to erode the work of the professionals who actually meet with, and have an ongoing relationship with, the investing public. Silicon Valley is helping them. Between Silicon Valley and Wall Street, they're convincing the public the advisor they go see every quarter, who takes the time to have a cup of coffee, and talks about their children and their grandchildren, the advisor they can ask, "When should I begin to take Social Security?" and the litany of things a financial advisor goes over that have nothing to do with returns, is stealing from them somehow.

Make no mistake, it is you and I against them—and it's me they would like to get rid of.

It feels to me like Wall Street is convincing the public this kind of personal interaction between client and advisor is a worthless transaction, that what an investor really needs to do to get ahead is slowly push that advisor out of the picture, that professional who had that cup of coffee with you, and who went to your kid's wedding. "Let's get rid of her, because she's really the problem!"

"You and I have a deal," Wall Street is telling everyone. "Now, you'll never meet 'us,' cause 'us' isn't a thing, we're a corporation. But we're really looking out for you."

They're slowly convincing many people, with the robo-advisor bullshit, which is what it really is, that they never need to talk to a human. That's what people, especially young people, have grown up hearing: that advisors are a joke and they shouldn't pay them, they shouldn't want them, they're not helpful, and they're just stealing your money.

I had lunch two days ago with a client of mine, a fairly wealthy attorney, who is very successful, and a very nice person. He and his wife worked their fingers to the bone for the last thirty plus years; they're getting ready to retire. It was his birthday, so I said, "Hey, want to go to lunch?" He replied, "Yeah, that would be really nice." We talked for about an hour and a half at lunch and never once did we talk about money. The entire conversation centered around his anxiety about retiring, about not getting a paycheck, and what he had done for 37 years, what it would mean to him mentally to step away, and what was he going to do with his time; what his wife thinks should happen to their house, and how she also has anxiety about her job and when to retire. At the end, I made a recommendation for him to read a book I had read. What is that worth? I don't know. But you're not going to be able to call the CEO of a large firm—he's not coming to lunch with you to talk about the human side of dealing with your money.

If a customer pays 1% to invest $100,000, $1,000 to somebody, the advisor—if she's lucky—is getting $500. Wall Street wants it. It's nothing more than that. As advisors, we are the front line, and we get a decent share of the revenue that's produced for doing all of the work. Yet they want to get rid of us. I heard a CEO once say, "Look, you guys aren't going anywhere, because if we could get rid of you, we would." On the one hand, I thought, "Well, that's very honest of you." But on the other, I thought, "What a jerk." This suit, who does nothing more than shuffle papers all day and fly on corporate jets, has just told all of us if he could get rid of us, he would!

What Wall Street has said is, "Make your advisor show what you're paying him!" Meanwhile, they're charging more than the advisor.

It's very much a message of, "Pay no attention to the men behind the curtain."

Best I can tell, the wizard has convinced many folks to turn a blind eye to the real "man behind the curtain."

Gold and Platform Trading Salesmen

You can see, on any given night on CNBC, an ad for a trading platform. There's always a really handsome, gray-haired gentleman sitting in front of a bunch of monitors with blinking red and green lights and charts, and he's clearly got the market figured out because of all these blinking lights! They will sell you this for $29.99, or you can go to a class. There are all kinds of pitches going on.

Or, you'll see a billboard: "TRADE YOUR WAY TO WEALTH. SEMINAR AT THE DOWNTOWN MARRIOTT NEXT FRIDAY."

My simple question to all the people behind these commercials and billboards is, if these trading platforms are foolproof ways to get rich, why aren't they just trading with them, then? Why are they trying to educate me for $499.00?

It's the same thing with gold. Back in '08 when the whole world was going to end, according to certain people, they were selling gold and saying, essentially, "This is the only known currency when things are terrible! When we're all road warriors and throwing rocks at each other, this is the thing." So, if I'm to understand the salesman correctly, the only currency that will exist that will be worth anything is these gold coins. Yet he would like to sell them to me for regular old American dollars. Seems odd.

If people just stopped for one second, and said, *What in the world?* But they don't.

Don't be a victim. It's a game of musical chairs, and you're probably not going to get a chair at the end.

Speaking of things to avoid, what do my eyes see but an E*TRADE ad? Seriously, an ad with a yacht in it and young beautiful people drinking Champagne!? Here is another one a few minutes later with a guy sitting hopelessly in coach (yes that *is* hopeless and uncomfortable) and longing for first class. These ads proclaim they have a trading platform that is not only "free," but will apparently allow you on in no time to trade your $5,000.00 savings account with such "amazing performance" that you too could be flying first class and dancing awkwardly on your $10 million yacht. Hurray!

My boring drivel is no longer needed. Wait? Where have these ads been prior to the recent market run? Why run these now, after five years when the magic trading ads have been largely missing? Ah sarcasm, I'd be lost without you.

It seems trading platform sales are and always will be based on the idea that you can trade on your own successfully and without much effort or experience. It is for this reason they wait until confidence is high in markets to start to rope you in. As you know, I am not in the habit of calling market tops, but these ads and the euphoria, not to mention the misplaced confidence they attach themselves to, are, in my 30 years of experience, often a sign that things are getting a tiny bit frothy.

To be clear, I am not saying that folks who use such services are not capable or even sometimes successful. What I am saying is that the more I see these ads preying on your desire to own a yacht, the more I start to think it's time to make sure I'm wearing a life preserver.

Driving Through the Smoke

I find there is no limit to the wisdom one can attain from NASCAR. In full disclosure, *Days of Thunder* ain't no *Talladega Nights, the Legend of Ricky Bobby*. With that wisdom under our helmets, let us consider one of the main lessons of stock car racing: drive through the smoke.

In *Days of Thunder,* Robert Duvall assures Tom Cruise he can drive through the smoke and come out the other side of the wreck, but if he hits the brakes or swerves he's gonna be part of the mess he's trying to avoid. What does that have to do with the price of tea in China, you may ask. NOTHING, that's my point. The price of tea in China, North Korea, Janet Yellen, Democrats, Republicans and alike are mostly smoke and no fire. I suggest you drive straight through.

In 30 years of doing business with the financially successful and not so successful, I have noticed one common thread in the former. They are, by and large, ignorant. What? Come again? Don't you mean the *unsuccessful* are ignorant? Nope. The successful are ignorant, but not in the traditional sense. Not in the "I don't read," or "I've lived in a cave for the last twenty years" kind of way. More in the, "Gosh, I wasn't aware that the economy was so bad when I started my multimillion-dollar business," or in a "I wasn't aware that tax policy was stacked against me when I opened my fourth profitable restaurant."

The term for this kind of ignorance/genius is "Selective Ignorance." The term refers to one's ability to drown out the noise or, for our purposes, drive through the smoke. With the advent of social media, there is smoke everywhere, often even when there is no wreck. Smoke from the media, smoke from your politically out-of-control Facebook friend, smoke from do-nothing politicians, smoke from your know-it-all brother-in-law. Smoke, but often no fire.

Sure, there are fires, but I got news for you: most of them are gonna burn whether you try to put them out or not. Allowing yourself to focus on the many wrecks, real or imagined, is a sure-fire way to end up on pit row wondering what happened in turn four. Economically successful people pay no attention to the spinning cars and/or the crowd longing for the dramatic. Kim Jong Un, China, Democrats, Republicans, aliens both illegal and from other planets, interest rates, and over-blown conspiracies are the tools of inaction.

Again, I'm not denying bad stuff happens. Tough! Turn off the TV and get to work on whatever it is you've been blaming the last three administrations for keeping you from. In short, mash the hell out of the accelerator and drive straight for the smoke, 'cause we all know, "If you ain't first, you're last."

Key Chapter 7 Takeaways:

- Do not overvalue the acronyms.
- Build a process.
- Beware the wolves who say what you want to hear.
- There is no insider information, and if you have it, it's illegal to use it anyway.
- Great advisors are good people, big picture people, who tell the truth.
- Be wary of Florida real estate.
- Don't be a victim.
- Be brave and drive through the smoke.

Chapter 8
What Comes After Success?

Age to me means nothing. I can't get old; I'm working. I was old when I was 21 and out of work. As long as you're working, you stay young. When I'm in front of an audience, all that love and vitality sweeps over me and I forget my age. ~George Burns

We were all convinced, back in the Depression Era when Social Security became a thing at 65, that sometime in your mid-60s, you should go sit in a chair and watch Perry Mason. First of all, everyone died on average by age 64 then. So, no one was supposed to get Social Security until they entered their nineties, which is another topic. The point is, we've been convinced to retire, and it's my firm belief human beings are not designed for that. Human beings are designed for constant growth and interaction and curiosity, and basically, *living*. Not sitting around. That's why I think depression is a problem. Anxiety is a problem.

Never before has a generation had the luxury to sit around and wonder what's going to go wrong. They were too busy killing the bear, planting the corn, dealing with the outbreak of smallpox, fighting wars, other tribes, deadly animals, snakes. They never had time to go, "I wonder why so-and-so hates me. Do I need Botox, is my caloric intake right?" This luxury is killing us.

We have a lot of elder depression, because people just shut down. If you're a high-powered lawyer or an engineer who is used to that kind of cognitive function on a regular basis, you can't just one day go, "Okay, now I'm gonna watch TV!" To go from a demanding and stimulating profession to *Jerry Springer*, it's not going to work!

They were sold: *you're going to get to relax, and you're going to get to do nothing.* The problem is, nothing SUCKS.

A lot of my clients volunteer, or they work part-time. I don't think I'll ever retire. I love entrepreneurship, I love starting businesses. I have plenty of charities to deal with, so I'll always have something to do; I think that's critical.

Happiness, once you reach sustenance, does not go up when you have more money.

It's not an accident that many retirees vote the way they vote—because they're angry, and they have angst about being retired. They don't earn income anymore, so they've lost control. They're really dependent on the government to some degree, so they're really angry at the government. I always say to my son, "You'll like me giving you money. You'll like it a lot, but there will come a time when you resent me for it because I will have kept you from that satisfaction and that sense of pride that comes from doing it yourself."

Because of what I do, I see this kind of resentment a lot. No matter how bad you are at earning money, there is a sense of pride that comes from it. So, I think when people retire and they give up the paycheck they were earning, it can make them angry at the entity that's giving them money.

I see it with trust fund kids who are now 50. They are as pissed off at the world, about the trust officer who won't give them the money when they want it: "I know I just got a car last year, but the new one's out and that's my money!" Well, actually, that's not your money. You may control it now, but you didn't earn it.

I see this with people who inherit money as well, which is why I don't like to work with them much. They can be the cheapest people who walk through that door, because A) they don't know how that money was made, and B) they know they can't remake it. So, they don't want to pay anybody anything—they're trying to hold onto it with both hands. Whereas the entrepreneur knows if it's all taken from him tomorrow, he'll go out and do it again. Of course, not all folks who inherit a bunch of money are in this category, but I do see it a lot. Now, before you get all huffy, most folks inherit "some" money. I'm referring to the previously broke individual who now has a large chunk of dough.

I can tell you, I know lots of wealthy people, and there are as many wealthy people who are unhappy whiners as people without money. The percentages do not change. Some of the most miserable sons-of-bitches I ever met in my life were wealthy.

As an experiment, I rented a house in the mountains of North Carolina once. I had really developed my business, to the way I thought I wanted it, and I decided that one of the things I was going to experiment with was time off. So, we (my wife, daughter and I) rented a house for a month on a lake to see how my staff did, and see how I did. I took my laptop and I was connected. The first week, I played three or four rounds of golf, worked on a crossword puzzle, read a book...but by day ten, I was climbing the walls. I didn't make it the whole month.

What was interesting about the experience was learning something about myself, and about retirement and leisure as well. On either side of me were multi-million-dollar homes. One neighbor in particular was nice enough, he was probably 71 or 72, a retired high-powered lawyer out of Atlanta. He had oodles of money. Well, best I could tell, every morning he got up, made himself a Bloody Mary and breakfast, played golf with two or three guys, played cards in the afternoon, drinking the whole time, and then went home, and made himself another drink. He invited me into this process for a while.

He was cordial, very polite, but he was miserable, you could just tell. He was inebriated, his energy was all sucked out of him, he didn't know what to do with himself. He could've done anything, he had all kinds of money, but what he did was sit around and drink. You know, I sat with him for a couple of hours at a time, and he was an interesting, smart guy. I think he went to Georgia undergrad and he might've gone to Vanderbilt Law, so obviously a bright guy. But he never really smiled, and he never really laughed. In the beginning, I was like, *this is fun!* But then the second or third time I hung out with him, I was like, *this is what he does every day?*

I'm a gregarious person, I can be silly with the best of them, but he just never laughed. He wasn't a jerk, but to me, he wasn't happy. Human beings need purpose. Idleness will not make you happy.

The New Retirement Is To...Not

In his book *The New Retirementality*, "unretirement" is the term Mitch Anthony uses to describe what people in their late 50s and early 60s are now doing.

That is...THEY ARE NOT JUST RETIRING! In the good ole days of your granddaddy, people retired in their 60s and were out of here like grease through a goose (I think you know what the real saying is) by 70 at the latest. In fact, as the New Deal came into being, the original thoughts were to make the age of "Entitlement" (their word, not mine. Murmur amongst yourselves) 70.

Now this, of course, was the 1930s, and folks generally lived to the ripe old age of 64; thus, not many were getting what was to be got. Today we know folks who are playing golf and jumping out of perfectly good airplanes at the age of 80 and above. In short, we're living longer. Another funny thing that happened along the way to modern day America is that the landscape of professions began to shift from industrial and agricultural back-breaking work to a service industry-based economy. Basically, we ain't all sitting out in the hot sun over a shovel like we used to.

This change in our economic base from building and making stuff out in the elements to taking turns selling and serving each other things in the air conditioning meant that people who reached their late 50s and early 60s were no longer as beaten up or broken down, on the whole, as they used to be.

For my part, my wife is convinced I talk on the phone and go to lunch for a living. I, of course, take issue with this as I clearly also go to dinner sometimes. That all said, we are now faced with an aging population that is not only NOT aging (thank you, Botox) to an after-60 crowd that is still able and ready to work. In fact, Anthony outlines in his book that nearly 40% of the U.S. labor force will reach traditional retirement age by 2020. What will they do? Will they plunge off the retirement cliff into a vicious circle of golf, reruns, and grumpiness?

In my business, I see all sides of the retirement program. I would suggest the term "retirement" is outdated and should be stricken from our vocabulary. Many of my clients today are not retiring, but redefining their work schedules for a bit more leisure and meaningful endeavors. I have one couple who each year picks a not-for-profit in some part of the country and spends six months working and six months at a fish hatchery or a national park clearing paths, usually getting food and lodging for free or at some deep discount. They are in their early 70s.

There is an air pocket of skilled workers coming up behind the baby boomers and it continues until you reach workers in their early 30s. The work these boomers do must still be done until the 30-somethings catch up.

Here comes the good news for those of you who fall into the skilled labor baby boomer demographic: you're going to get to call the shots. More and more companies are setting up systems to use "unretired" workers and their expertise on a project-by-project basis. The good news is you take what you want. You golf when you don't.

Recently I was having dinner (ugh...she's right) with an eye surgeon client of mine. I was sharing with him the "New Retirementality" as outlined in Anthony's book. He said, "Wait, let me get this straight. I should be able to do the surgery I love when and if I want and make someone else do the paperwork and annoying administrative stuff?" BINGO!

While this will not work perfectly for everyone, I suspect more and more of you will "unretire" in the near future. Until then...give me a call, we'll do lunch.

Ergodicity

I know what you're thinking: *he's run out of things to talk about* (fat chance), *and he's stooped to making up words.* While I understand the sentiment, "ergodicity" is a real word and the title of researcher and author Luca Dellana's recently released book.

Simply put, ergodicity is the study of a broad range of systems that occur in physics and geometry. Don't panic, there's a simpler way to understand the concept, and this rural Florida bumpkin loves him some simple. Ergodics, for our purposes, is *the study of survivability:* the survivability of us as humans and more importantly, the survivability of the community and the species. We'll apply it to the survival of your wealth.

Some folks say that Warren Buffet is a genius. Some say he's been lucky or has dogged determination and grit. I say, *he is old.* Now, before you get all offended, I suspect he knows he is old and I am not dismissing the many skills he has. That all said, many folks are smart and tenacious, but have nowhere near the financial success of Warren. (We're on a first-name basis, of course.) What Warren has, in addition to a strong acumen for investing, is an ergodic approach to life. To survive is to thrive. Two-thirds of his wealth was gathered after he had reached the age of 60.

What does this have to do with us non-billionaires? A lot, I would argue. Many folks who have made and accumulated a decent amount of wealth struggle once their careers come to an end and they are now tasked with maintaining the money. Author Morgan Housel is fond of saying that "accumulating wealth" and "maintaining wealth" are two very different skill sets.

Maintaining wealth is purely a matter of survival. I have this much money and I need it to produce income or supplement my retirement over the next 30 years if I'm lucky. Many folks think this process is the same as making and saving money. It is not. Making and saving money is about full on narrow and non-diverse thinking.

I'm all in on my education as a ____ (your profession here), or going hard into the savings mode in my 401k and or other similar vehicles. If you had not fully narrowed your focus and energy, you would likely not have saved the money you did or sold the business that has now resulted in the wealth you now need to preserve.

Maintaining wealth is where "ergodic thinking" becomes critical. To succeed is to survive – plain and simple.

In his book, Luca describes a situation with his cousin, who was a downhill skier. The cousin was, without a doubt, the fastest skier in his community. The problem with his cousin was that he also was never the most successful skier, primarily because he was often hurt due to the reckless nature of his skiing. In short, he was fast, but he was not successful. He did not survive practice rounds or preliminary races to get to the championships. Luca's cousin was not "ergodic" in his approach.

To continue the analogy, many of you think you want the fastest time, or in this case the highest return, so you pivot to every headline stock or idea that you think will get you to the bottom of the hill the fastest. What you don't realize is you can win the championship not by skiing slowly or investing overly conservatively, but by skiing or investing just fast enough to excel, but more importantly, to survive.

History is full of fast skiers: Enron, subprime mortgages, tulips, dot com stocks, and, most recently, meme stocks. Skiing fast or investing aggressively are more than okay when done within an ergodic framework. Buying the "hot crypto" or your brother's stock is fine, as long as you have an ergodic base to allow for that stock to tank or for that brush with the gate halfway down the mountain.

If you have 80% of your money built for survivability and the avoidance of ruin, you're good to go on the crazy crypto idea of the day. It's when folks get out over their skis and go all in that ruin is a factor. Ruin can NEVER be an option for a retiree or even a late-stage pre-retiree. Ruin is game over; ruin is back to work greeting folks at Wal-Mart. Once ruin is removed from your options (as best we can do that), getting up on an occasional edge to gather speed is okay and, in fact, ideal.

In short (too late, I know) we must first design our run and determine how we survive before we can determine how to excel. The former is 90% of attaining the latter.

Why is American Capitalism Winner Take All?

It's a very third-world mentality that we're leaning back into, and it's not good. People walk into Best Buy and they'll say, "Oh that TV is $1,249? Amazon has it for $1,100," and they leave. To hell with the salesman and the people who mop the floors and the person who hung the TV. That's how we think now; I see it every day.

Not very often, but occasionally, a person will walk in here, drink my Coke, talk to my secretary, give papers to my assistant to organize, ask me a thousand questions, and are honestly pissed off they have to pay me. They believe I should do this for free. Now, they don't do whatever it is *they* do for free. There is a firm belief in this country that everybody else is overpaid, but you, of course, are underpaid. I don't know when we turned that corner, where we felt the need to get over on each other.

It seems like everyone wants to start with a fair deal that benefits both parties and then see how much more they can get. I don't know how it happened, but it's not good, and it's not good for all of us.

Corporate America is excellent at this because they have lobbying power. If you have a small appliance shop, you can't go to your Senator and say, "Here's a cupcake, keep me in mind when you do legislation," because Amazon has given that guy a hundred grand. He doesn't care about you, and he'll *never* care about you. The lobbying thing is just a complete mess. I don't know how we're going to fix that. American capitalism is not a pretty thing anymore. I actually don't want to play, because you have to be mean even if you don't want to be.

The Rewards of Building a Business

I've succeeded as an advisor because I love people. People piss me off like anybody else, but I love getting a postcard from Alaska from my client, and I love having dinner with one of my doctors and talking about the fact that he just went to Tanzania. I love the people part of it, helping my clients ground themselves. They don't do what I do every day, so it would be stupid to assume they get it on the level I get it. But if I can bring my experience to the table for them and say, "You know that's ridiculous, we've talked about this," I can help steer them away from bad financial decisions.

It's like, when I go to the doctor, I don't feel good, I'm nervous. But he can say, "Relax, man. It's just a *whatever*." I'm uptight about it, but they're completely relaxed because they have the expertise.

That's what I want to provide my clients with, in the money arena. We all have our role to play, but it's still a people thing.

What I also love is the business of business, though most advisors don't—most advisors want to be employees deep down inside. I, on the other hand, love talking to business owners about their companies. We talk about staff issues, the numbers for the year, economics, construction problems, the whole gamut of issues owners face. I have clients that I talk to about my business. In my CEO group, it amazes me that we are in 17 different businesses, but 90 percent of the issues are common: staff, HR, technology. You name it, it's all the same stuff.

When you grow a business, now 23 people have jobs. That wasn't just me, but I had a hand in it. I'm going to our Christmas party, and I was just informed there are going to be 55 people there! Part of it is intimidating, part of it is exciting.

I know people right this second who are business owners who have not taken a paycheck in six months so they didn't have to fire anybody. Capitalism certainly isn't perfect, but capitalists are not bad, self-serving people.

Meaning, Struggle, Reward

I recently listened to the Patrick Smith classic *A Land Remembered*, the fictional story of a family named the McIveys who made their way down the Kissimmee River Basin to build a life for themselves as the Civil War was winding down. I am a fourth generation native Floridian, and the tale reminds me of growing up before Time Sharing, the mouse, hanging chads, and air conditioning in my elementary school (OMG). It reminds me of fishing in the mangroves and hunting rabbits in Pasco County (sorry, Grandma).

If you have any affection for the fair state of Florida, and you're not just stopping by to be governor or something (sorry...couldn't resist), you'll enjoy the book. The business lessons that one can take from the characters and their never-quit attitude is worth remembering. In the novel, the McIveys, led by their patriarch Tobias, start out by hunting and foraging in the swamps and eventually gather enough stray cows originally left behind by the Spanish to build a reasonable cattle business.

As time goes on, the McIveys grow as a family and a business, experiencing both success and tremendous hardship. From wild animals to rustlers, their "investment" in the land and themselves on numerous occasions seems certain to fail. Each and every time their herd is decimated or a family member tragically dies (which was very common in those days), the McIveys press on, understanding there was no other option.

Back then, businessmen and women like the McIveys knew success or failure, more correctly life or death, was determined by their will to succeed and overcome temporary failure. What the heck does this have to do with investing? Well, nothing and everything. I have recommended to the young people in my practice they listen to (or get crazy and actually read) the Patrick Smith classic because, like the McIveys' epic struggle to survive and eventually prosper, all investors will encounter difficulties in their hopefully long journey.

I have heard numerous people, both regular Joes as well as known pundits proclaim, "I will never invest again" after various economic calamities. Similar to Tobias McIvey buying orange trees for his farm after the big freeze of 1894 (remember that?), Warren Buffett and other determined investors soldier on and prosper while others wither in the face of adversity.

Investing in anything, yes ANYTHING, has risk. The real risk is in giving up when things get tough, which is another way of saying...right before things have the potential to get better.

Key Chapter 8 Takeaways:

- It's time to rethink retirement. Don't check out of life.
- There's pleasure to be found in building something, particularly a business.
- If you feel angry all the time, turn off the news.
- Let's pull back from the winner-take-all mentality.
- Don't give up when things get tough.

Section Two
Products & Practical Tips

Chapter 9
How to Work with An Advisor

There is no future without a plan.

Expectations are for fools. As they say in sports, "Let the game come to you." Sure, we all have hopes and dreams, and sure, we all have a lifetime of experiences that point us in a specific direction. That said, if your investment compass is so accurate, it is likely you wouldn't be sitting in the office of a financial expert, now would you?

When you go to see an advisor, I would pay attention to who the hero is. Spoiler alert: you're the hero. If the advisor spends thirty minutes explaining how great they are and why you will likely name your next child after them, I would start looking for the exit. What *should* be happening is a whole hell of a lot of listening.

The advisor should be asking questions like: "What have you done in the past that you liked, and what have you done in the past that you ended up not liking—and why?"

Sure, it's great that the guy in the fancy suit has an MBA, CFP™, and is a licensed Cosmetologist, but none of that is worth a hill of beans if he won't shut up and listen. Once, after many years of suffering from a balance issue, I was referred to an Ear, Nose, and Throat doc who was considered the most credentialed dude in his business. He burst into my examining room with a young resident and asked me what the issue was without so much as a "Hi, my name is Dr. Awesome. How are you?"

He asked what seemed to be the issue. I replied, a little sheepishly, "Do you have time for a story?" His answer was, "Not a long one."

Well, as you can imagine, that went over like a turd in a punch bowl. I gave Dr. Jackass and his sidekick a two second "I'm dizzy" story and got out of his office as fast as I could. The moral of the story is that your advisor must be an "A" number one badass at listening. They must listen and take notes. They must listen and ask short but thoughtful questions. We have two ears and one mouth...you do the math.

To reiterate, when you go see an advisor for the first time, you should have no expectations. You can't go in with the thought, *this is what they're going to do for me,* because you're likely to be wrong. Every advisor has a thing they like to do, or a way they like to do it, things they are biased toward, and things they are biased against. I try desperately not to be that guy, but we all do it, we're all human beings.

I try to prod new clients. I might get an engineer who doesn't want to talk; he's waiting for me to say what my algorithm is, my "X + Y = I'm rich" formula. But I don't have one of those, unfortunately. I say, "Tell me about your past experiences. Tell me what you liked, tell me what you didn't like. You're obviously here for a reason, what is it?" I let them talk.

What I'm trying to figure out when they're talking to me is what bad habits and ideas their brains are filled with, and how far gone they are with the nonsense that's pushed on people day in and day out. I'm trying to figure out, *can I fix it? Will it stay fixed once I do?* Because sometimes people will initially agree, "You're right, you're right, this is nonsense, I shouldn't react this way, I shouldn't do this," and three weeks later, they do something impulsive again.

So, I'm trying to gauge, is this person hanging on too tight, is this going to be combative? Are their expectations crazy?

Clients will often say, "You will tell me when to get out, right?" One of my favorite things to do is reply, "I have no idea how to do that," and watch the expression on their faces.

I'll tell you when to get in: when you have the money. You buy quality things so getting out isn't as important. That's not to say we shouldn't mitigate the risks or do things to make the ride a little bit less bumpy, but the ride is going to be bumpy from time to time.

You have to feel a click at that first meeting. The thing I would be most leery of is the product push right away. I don't even bring up what we're investing in, usually, at the first meeting with a new client. I want to see if they're serious. If they're serious, they'll come back for the good stuff.

To be a client of mine is work. It requires homework, fact-finding, it requires giving me details, and I don't have time to chase you for four months. If my staff has to call you seven times, and you break three appointments, that's costing me a fortune. I can't have that, I need to make sure a new client is willing to put in the work and hold me accountable. I want somebody who is a partner.

Look for an advisor who is willing to spend time with you, who is writing down what you say, who is really paying attention to your concerns, rather than just waiting to show you a brochure.

The first meeting, just go in and talk as people. You could say, "If I come back, what should I bring?" My team sends out specific instructions if I have a good first meeting with a potential client.

Someone on my team will send out an email: *here's your homework*. Then, within about ten days, we know if they're legit. Generally, the legit people get everything back to us in four or five days; the non-so legit people take much longer, in which case I get bored and say, forget it.

I wouldn't bring anything to the first meeting other than the willingness to be honest about your concerns.

The Whole Truth and Nothing but the Truth

The first thing you should do when you work with a financial advisor is commit yourself to honesty. People don't want to say much, they don't want to tell an advisor much…but that means you're going to get half of a solution. It's happened to me, even though I'm usually pretty good at telling when someone's fibbing. I'll say, "Tell me what you have and what you're trying to accomplish." "Well, I've got $200,000 in a brokerage account at Chase." "Okay, cool, anything else?" "Not really." Then I find out three months later when they come back in they have $600,000 in an E*TRADE account that has lost money every year for the last four. It's usually the guy who doesn't want to divulge that. Dudes are funny that way.

I've gotten to the point in my career where I don't really need more clients. I still want them, particularly if they are cool people, but I don't need them. I can afford to be honest. Twenty-four-year-old Scott could not afford to tell people tough stuff, but 50-something Scott definitely can and will. Your advisor needs to be comfortable pushing back or that advisor will be of no use to you when things get tough…and things will get tough.

Often, a client will come in with preconceived ideas about what they want to keep or get rid of in a portfolio. So, I'll say, "Let me make sure I understand this: you want to pay me to keep losing money in the stocks you already own? Am I getting that right?" A lot of times this is a make-or-break moment with a potential client. The decision to really let go is a tough one, and if you can't, I cannot help you, nor can any other advisor worth a crap.

The truth is that if you were so good at buying and selling securities, you would not be in an advisor's office. Do you really want to keep paying someone to keep the same crappy stocks you couldn't make money in? We both know you're going to blame the advisor if things don't go well, so you might as well let them do something.

For me, it would be a warning sign if the advisor is okay with keeping all the crap you came in with. It tells me they do not have an existing discipline and that their primary interest is in charging you on your existing assets.

Be Picky

I would only give my money to one in ten advisors, maybe two in ten. Especially if you are an entrepreneur, and a lot of people who have money are entrepreneurial in one way, shape, or form. Entrepreneurs are always thoughtful and hard working. They take risks every day and can spot a slacker a mile away. You know the value of trust and, to some degree, the value of luck. Most advisors do not. They come to work at 9:30 and they get their coffee, they read *The Wall Street Journal,* and they go home at 4:00. Then, they can't figure out why the guy who just sold his plumbing company for $7 million has no interest in giving his money to them. Because he called at 4:30, and you were gone!

If you're with an advisor now, and you've been with that person for a while, you have a pretty good idea of who they are. If you've been with an advisor for ten years, and they're not scheduling regular meetings, and they're not making you do things you don't want to do, that's a red flag.

If an advisor is only telling you what you want to hear, you should fire him or her immediately, because what you want to hear is nonsense. What you want is your brilliant ideas reinforced, most of which are not brilliant. You need honesty and pushback when appropriate. If your spouse cares about you, and you're going to walk out of the house in a polka dotted shirt with striped pants, and they don't tell you, that's not very helpful. Not that I've done that.

You know in your heart if your advisor is working hard for you, or if the last time you heard from that person was when they needed a signature two years ago. If you have money, you likely have good instincts. Trust them.

Mistakes People Often Make with Advisors

There are a couple of very common mistakes people make going into a relationship with their financial advisor.

They think the advisor can make them rich, for one. For two, they make a lot of wild, inaccurate assumptions: an advisor knows what the market's going to do, she knows when it's going to do it, or he knows when to get in the market and when to get out of the

market (whatever "the market" is, there are multiple markets). The advisor knows which sector is going to be hot, which company is going to double their earnings, which stock is Facebook and which stock is Snapchat.
We don't know.

It's impossible for us to know the inner workings of IBM. Or which accountant at XYZ Corporation is actually skimming off the top, and when the scandal is going to break. How would we know that? We *don't* know that stuff.

While a trainer can't lift weights for you, a trainer does know what you need to do. Frankly, *you* know what you need to do, but you're not doing it. I go to a trainer, and I have many times over the years because I just wanted a new approach, or somebody to be accountable to, even though I know how to lift weights. I know how to run on a treadmill, and I know how to do push-ups. Despite all of those facts, sometimes I just wouldn't do it, for whatever made-up reason in my head: *Well, I went yesterday.* Or, *I did it last Tuesday,* or *my toe hurts today,* or whatever. Facts are, humans can be lazy or unmotivated. Like a trainer, you need an advisor to hold you accountable and vice versa.

An advisor is there to coach you, to counsel you, and to shorten the learning curve.

A client calls me up and says, "Scott, I need to take a hundred grand out of my accounts, what's the best way to do it?" They could figure that out. They could Google tax implications, and probably a few hours later, figure it out. Or, they could call me or text me for that answer in a minute. When something's wrong or a form needs to be filled out, they don't want to call a 1-800 number and hope the right form gets to them in five business days. They want my talented and trustworthy associate Linda to email it to them. That's what my clients do and it's what you should do.

There is nothing wrong with using discount trading platforms or "do it yourself" type systems. Some people enjoy this; some people like working on their own plumbing and fixing their own car. The problem is, most people are bad at this stuff and end up wasting a lot of time and money doing things wrong in an effort to "save" money. When it comes to wealth management, people are, more often than not, wrong about their prowess.

The people who use me value their time and value a level of expertise they don't have, and don't want to attain.

Yesterday, I was on a call with a client of mine. He and his wife are both lawyers; they're worth two or three million dollars. He said, "The IRS says I owe them $50 grand." He's talking to me like I did something wrong. I replied, "What do you mean? What does your accountant say?" He admitted, "I don't use an accountant. I do it myself." *The guy is worth $3 million.*

I was comfortable we had not caused his problem and knew that the $300.00 he likely saved by doing his own taxes might be about to cost him 50 large! I told him I knew we didn't send the IRS anything to lead them to the conclusion that he owed $50,000, so he needed to look where he did his taxes and let me know if these certain boxes were checked. As they say in football, "After further review, the cheapskate missed a box."

It nearly cost him $50,000! Had he not been able to turn to me to walk him through that situation, he would've just paid it! He called the IRS back and they said, "Okay, we'll fix this." Unfortunately, it's still going to cost him $5,000, which is probably ten times what he would've paid an accountant. Moreover, what is the value of not having that kind of headache in the first place?

People have been convinced and conditioned, by the media, by legislators, by politicians, by cut-rate discount shops to believe paying for professional services is ludicrous, that paying for someone's expertise is ludicrous. *You can do everything yourself,* they tell us. Really? So, you're going to do your own legal work? Your own accounting?

People don't value their own time. At all. I once had a friend tell me that he didn't need to worry about the cost of his time because he did all his planning in his "free" time. Free time!?

I don't know about you, but I value my "free" time at twice the rate I value my "work" time.

Working with an Advisor as One Half of a Couple

It can be tough. A lot of times, two people in a relationship have different ideas about what should be done. I try to figure out who is wearing the pants, but that can change so it's not a big deal to me. There's usually one person with anxiety, and I have to figure out what those anxieties are.

You'd be amazed at the things people say. They do get comfortable, they do talk to me about their differences, and they'll bicker in front of me. It happens; sometimes it gets a little awkward, but it's fine. I mean, who doesn't love a good spat? Money is really good at starting them.

I just kind of let them go through their natural conversation, because you know they're having it at home, too. Often there's a lot of anxiety because people, particularly husbands, are nervous they're not where they should be financially. The wives, who are often also powerful professionals, will be the ones who say, "We need to take the plunge, we've got to bare our souls."

Surprisingly enough, when we finally dig down into the details, we often find they are not nearly as bad off as they thought.

The path is very achievable, in most cases. So, the wives are often immensely relieved that they can now look up and see a spreadsheet, a path where they need to go. In the husbands' cases, they are usually relieved to find out they aren't the complete screw-ups they thought they were.

There's always this perception when people are referred to me by their friends or acquaintances that I'm going to be comparing people, comparing their net worth—but there's never that big of a discrepancy. Birds of a feather flock together.

Don't Get Caught Up in Alphabet Soup

Some of the biggest idiots I know have CFPs™ and MBAs, not that those are bad things. They're certainly nice things, but a lot of times people get too caught up in that stuff, particularly in my business. Some of the biggest jackasses who are in jail for stealing money from people have MBAs and CFPs™. To me, it's really about: do you click with the advisor, or not? I have strong opinions about my profession and what I do. I can't imagine that you would want to work with somebody who didn't.

Look for a willingness to work. I can't say this enough. I may not know what the market's going to do, I may not know what the president's going to do, especially now, but I promise you I'm going to work hard. I'm going to answer your phone calls when you call, whether I want to talk to you or not, because the market's down and I know what you *need* to hear, not necessarily what you *want* to hear. I'm going to make sure you get that form you want, and if you'd like to stop by and have a cup of coffee, I'm right here. You need to see me on a Saturday morning and I can do it? I will make that happen if it's necessary.

The ball will get dropped, mistakes get made, and I don't want to work with people who don't understand that, yet I tell my staff, "We never say to a client, 'we don't do that.'" The answer better be, "We can sort of do that, and we'll figure it out." You must hold your advisor accountable for things that are, in fact, accountable: hard work, professionalism and honesty. Things that you cannot hold them accountable for? MARKETS!

Financial advisors, just like individuals in any profession, are not all the same. People have a different level of commitment that they bring to their work. Some people are just waiting for time to pass. As an employee, the passage of time is your friend. As an entrepreneur, the passage of time is your enemy, because you can't get things done if the days are going by underneath you too quickly. If you've got an advisor who is just showing up at 9:30, you should be able to figure that out pretty quickly. If you can't figure that out, you're going to get what you deserve. If you're lazy about holding your advisor's feet to the fire, and they don't return your phone calls, that's on you. You have to seek out the good ones, because I promise you in every town there are a dozen who are really good at what they do.

Whenever I go to a conference for financial advisors, if there are 2,000 people there, the bottom 1,950 of them are competitive, over-dressed, over-consuming paranoid assholes. They are just peacocks. The top 50 are the kindest, most thoughtful, most interested-in-you types of folks in the world. They are the most "What can I do to help you?" kinds of people you'll ever meet. It's amazing to me how sharing they are, and how willing they are to learn, and how interested they are in what others have to say.

Meanwhile, the jackass with the custom cufflinks knows everything and thinks everything is stupid. I wish this weren't true, but it is obnoxiously true.

The most successful people in my industry are thoughtful, kind people. They read, they're into other things, they can quote poetry, they've been around the world, they've done a mission trip. Look for those people.

Understand What Your Financial Planner Is Doing

- Reject the jargon.
- Break out the crayons.
- Ask the dumb questions.

If you're like me, you often feel like you are anything but the smartest person in the room. I feel this way all the time, even when it's just me and the dog. We have all been to one of those "business" meetings where someone is talking way over our heads and using jargon that we don't understand and are embarrassed to ask about.

After many years in this business and the requisite one thousand meetings or so, I have really come to think folks in my field, and in many industries for that matter, lean on jargon and/or pretentious business slang to disguise the fact that they themselves really have no idea what they are talking about or, more correctly, don't really believe the pitch they are giving you.

If you are going to put your hard-earned dollars into an investment of any kind, the first thing I would require is an explanation that leans more toward Andy Griffith and less toward Stephen Hawking. Don't get me wrong, I dig a good debate on gravitational singularity theorems as much as the next Joe. That said, I will not be writing any checks for any investment, as Peter Lynch once said, "that I can't illustrate with a crayon."

Far too often, I sit across the table from a person who has suffered losses in an account they have no understanding of. I have many times heard the following: "Well, the guy just sounded so smart and he had all kinds of acronyms behind his name, so I figured he knew what he was doing."

In 1994, a group of Nobel Laureates (aka, smart guys), including PhDs Myron Scholes and Robert Merton, formed a hedge fund called Long Term Capital Management. Not only were these dudes smart, they had Nobel Prizes for their work in finance, which reeks of greatness.

Well, as you might imagine, folks tripped over themselves to give these geniuses their money, wowed by complex mathematical models and terms like "fixed income arbitrage" and "convergence trades." I mean, heck, if you can't trust two PhD havin', Nobel Prize winnin', algorithm spoutin' bona fide smart guys, WHO CAN YOU TRUST?

Well, it turns out...not Merton and Scholes. In 1998, LTCM wiped out north of $4 billion worth of wealth during the Asian and Russian Financial Crisis, and had to be subsequently bailed out by a consortium of banks organized by the Federal Reserve. In short, we bailed them out and they, along with many of their "sophisticated" clients, lost billions. The lesson, again, is that many of us are guilty of shying away from what we believe are dumb questions.

After all, as my first boss used to say, "It's better to sit quietly and let people think you're an idiot than to open your mouth and remove all doubt." Why he said this to me repeatedly is still a bit confusing. We are all afraid of looking silly, especially when in the company of more informed and seemingly more intelligent people seeking our money. Still, financial transactions are not the place to hesitate if you have questions. If someone is asking for your hard-earned money, they should be prepared to break out the crayons.

Streaky Forks

If you haven't seen the new series *The Bear,* I highly recommend it. It's a compelling story of a Chicago restauranter and chef who is both a culinary genius and slightly disturbed. I can relate...to the latter, not the former.

What, pray tell, does this have to do with money or investing? good question. As most of you know my son Bracher (Brat-chur; don't worry, he's used to repeating it and yes, it's a family name) is now three years in with the firm and becoming an intricate part of my plan to play more golf and generally goof off.

I bring him up because he, like his father, has a propensity for seeing links between pop culture and this business we call "investing." In this case, he shared in our Monday morning team meeting a clip from the aforementioned television show. In the clip, one of the main characters (Richie) was having a heated discussion with the newly hired manager about quality control and the importance or lack thereof of streaky forks. Hang on, I'm getting there.

Richie, a holdover from the restaurant's more rugged and greasier past, was arguing that slightly streaky forks were inconsequential and that no one would notice. Of course, the high-end manager who had recently been hired shared a different view. This view, to summarize, was that many of the folks who came to their restaurant had maybe saved for months to be able to afford to eat there. They had maybe hired a babysitter or bought a new outfit for the occasion. Maybe they had recently experienced some tough times and this dinner out was a moment to relax and live for an hour or two free from problems. In fact, this meal was supposed to be a break from life's often harsh realities.

He, in no uncertain terms, made it clear that when these people picked up their forks that evening, the slightest streaks would in some way remind them of that which they were escaping, even if just for a couple of hours.

So, yes Richie, clean the #@*^% forks!

As always, you must now be wondering what this has to do with our relationship and the world that is my business and your economics. My son's well-made point in playing this clip was that everything matters. We as your advisors must make sure our forks aren't streaky and that from the second we engage with you, we are engaged.

My team and I reemphasize weekly that every person who walks through our door has a story. Often, if not always, this story has difficult twists and turns, disappointments, and heartache.

Often it has involved years (decades) of hard work and moments of complete frustration, if not despair. All our clients are what many would call "successful" and or "wealthy." We remind ourselves every day that "success" is not born of just luck. To be fair, luck plays a role, but so do perseverance and effort. We try to remember that we're only seeing the glorious part of the struggle, but hopefully we are showing you every day that we recognize and respect that you've chosen to entrust us with the rewards of that struggle.

We thank you for dining with us and if ever you see a fork that needs shining, please let us know. After 36 years in this business, I think my passion (weird, I know) for providing a better and more meaningful experience to our clients has only grown stronger.

Do You Feel Money Shame or Money Embarrassment?

You're not alone—that's most people. Most 50-year-olds have done almost nothing when it comes to financial planning for their futures. They might have a 401(k), and they might have $30,000 in an IRA or whatever, and they might have $10,000 they inherited, and feel embarrassed about not being further along. But the longer you wait to take a close look at your situation, the less chance you have of making it better.

I recently had a couple come in who I'd been after for a year because they're friends of friends of mine, and I almost immediately sensed that the reason one of the two hadn't wanted to come in for a meeting with me was because he wasn't where he wanted to be. In his mind, he was going to *get* to where he wanted to be *before* he came to see me—like trying to get in better shape before going to see a trainer.

Finally, they came in, and it's been awesome. When someone feels a bit hesitant about working with an advisor yet comes in to see me anyway, 90% of the time I find out that they're not as badly off as they think they are. I am able to give them better news than they expect. That's not to say that this couple, and probably most people, don't have work to do, but just *understanding* the work you have to do is half, if not three-quarters, of the battle. Just show up, and we'll build a plan.

Money shame? Get over it.

Get with a financial advisor, and don't make the decision of who to work with based on a TV ad. Poll your friends, your wealthier friends and your humble friends, to find out who they're working with. I always find it funny when someone comes in with some foolish scheme and says, "Well, my brother or my aunt or whoever says I should do *this*." I always say, "Well, are they well off?" The answer is often no. So, what makes you think they know what they're talking about? Go to people you respect when polling for an advisor—people who are thoughtful, successful, and humble.

Financial planners are everywhere, which is a good thing and a bad thing. Most of them are worthless; they're salespeople in disguise. There's less of that than there used to be, but there's still a bunch of it, which is why those personal recommendations are so important. Someone should take the time to get to know you, not sell you some predetermined thing they think you need before you even start to talk. For your part, you should be willing to compensate them. People say, "Well, that comes out of my return!"

To which I say, "You don't even *have* a return now. You're not doing what you're supposed to be doing." 100% of nothing is still nothing.

Is a Bull Market a Quick Fix? NO!

Whenever people walk into an advisor's office, whether it's mine or somebody else's, they're looking for a quick fix. They're asking, more or less, "How can I get my master's degree in four weeks?" That's what they think they're looking for: "Well, my guy is really smart, and he bought me Microsoft, and it went up 40 percent."

Well, okay, that might've happened, but that was also probably a fluke. That's not our job. If you think it's our job, you're going to be sorely disappointed at some point. Markets determine outcomes as far as returns go, but "never confuse a bull market with brilliance," as Warren Buffett once said. Everybody thinks they're a genius today because the market's been going up for years.

I had a young man sitting in my office this morning tell me how awesome he was doing day trading. I said, "How did you do in 2008?" He said, "Oh, I was, like, 12 then." So, I said, "Okay, come see me when 2008 happens again so we can determine exactly how smart you are, because right now a monkey with a dart is pretty smart."

S#&! Rolls Downhill

In 2008, what you saw was that the marginal people in our business who were just salespeople couldn't sell. The story wasn't good: "This investment is down 15%, would you like to buy it?" Mutual fund providers sell mutual funds based on last year's returns; because of that, the bad returns of 2007-2009 saw a lot of people leave the advisory business. We saw a lot of people in the industry speed up their retirements. They were just over it, they didn't want to go through another bear market. For my part, I've got one more in me, one more downturn that I can live with. Because it's tough; it's tough on advisors. Shit rolls downhill, and we're the stopping point.

Some clients will leave when the going gets rough, because they will blame you. That's why I'm very careful to point out that this up market isn't my doing. We try to position them, to put them in processes and places and give them opportunities to succeed. Then, when things are not so great, we try to counsel them on how not to make mistakes they'll regret: "Okay, that stock looks terrible, let's get out of that. But *that's* just a product of the environment, don't get out of that." So, my job during a downturn is a lot of counseling, it's a lot of hand-holding.

It's the opposite now, in this bull market. Everybody wants to be more aggressive now. "I could probably earn 30%!" They tell me. Well, yeah, but you could also get your head lopped off. Don't get too greedy.

There's a whole different tone when things are down. Clients will lie to you, straight to your face. They'll say, "Oh, if it drops 10%, I'm not going to worry about it." Then they'll blow up my phone once it does. Because, as Mike Tyson famously says, everyone's got a plan until they get punched in the face. My favorite saying is *people are okay with volatility as long as it's up.*

Financial Planning: A Play in 15 Acts

The following are my notes from my meeting this morning with Dr. Daniel Jones and his wife, Cynthia Jones:

1. We discussed the overall economy and the market forecasts of firm strategists.

2. I shared forecasts for the year ahead from both a technical and fundamental standpoint.

3. We agreed that markets seemed at least initially inspired by recent political events, but to be cautious of overexuberance.

4. We went through each account, holding by holding, evaluating performance versus the appropriate indexes. We agreed the few that were not outperforming their indexes should remain due to the cyclical nature of the markets, but that further monitoring was in order.

5. We reviewed our asset allocation and the appropriateness of it going forward. In doing so, we reviewed their statistical likelihood of a potential positive return (as defined by them) and determined the needed ratio of fixed income to equities (stocks) was in keeping with the current mix.

6. We agreed that, due to their projected retirement date, we should begin evaluating the need for dividend production versus growth sometime late next year as a

means of helping to provide income without invading principle.

7. We agreed that, due to their net worth, long-term care insurance made some sense and would likely protect their estates should those services become necessary.

8. We agreed that we should all meet with their estate attorney in the months ahead to confirm that the distribution of assets will be done as they intend, as it has been nearly six years since they revisited that issue. Their children are now grown and priorities have changed a bit with grandchildren in the picture.

9. We added a 529 account to their portfolio for their youngest grandchild.

10. We reviewed life insurance, and agreed they were well covered at this point. They will lose a substantial amount of coverage in two years due to a term policy expiring; thus, we agreed to continue discussions on that need in the months ahead.

11. We reviewed Dr. Jones' current 401(k) and Profit Sharing Plan to make sure the allocation was in keeping with our stated objectives for risk and return.

12. We reviewed all fees, both here with us and in his company retirement plans. This review was not only of advisory fees, but of the products themselves, as Dr. Jones had no idea what he was paying prior to doing so.

13. We reviewed Cynthia's Profit Sharing Plan as well, from ABC Defense Contractors, as she is an engineer there and will likely work part time beyond 2018.

14. Cynthia enjoys the Market Watch report we do on individual issues and we have agreed to send that to her on a regular basis.

15. We covered the most beneficial scenario for receiving Social Security, which calls for her to take a spousal benefit until she reaches full retirement age, and then convert to her own benefit.

The following are my notes from my meeting with Laura and Ben Johnson:

1. They are young, but enthusiastic about saving. Laura's parents suggested they come in and, to their credit, they listened.

2. They don't have a lot in assets, but are good savers, especially for a couple in their late 20s.

3. Laura is a saver and Ben is not far behind with a slight addiction to motorcycles. (Who can blame him?)

4. She is a physician assistant now in her third year, and he is an engineer at a local defense contractor.

5. They both have 401(k)s and will be providing those statements.

6. She has a small inheritance in a discount brokerage account, which she will provide in our discovery process.

7. They have not purchased a house but are considering using the inheritance for that purpose. On the surface, this seems logical.

8. They just found out Laura is pregnant and want to start a College Saving program and mentioned a 529. We will review the cost of state and out of state tuition, and provide guidance on saving, both in a 529 and a state-sponsored tuition program.

9. They want to run a spreadsheet on ROTH versus Traditional IRAs.

10. They have a small term policy on Ben, but obviously with the pending birth of their first, insurance is more of a priority.

11. They asked for, and we provided, the firm's summary of recent tax legislation and what it may mean to them.

12. She gave us their CPA's number so that we could reach out if necessary.

13. We have sent them home with a few questions in preparation for our next and more intensive planning meeting.

14. We will reach out shortly to schedule that meeting.

The preceding reviews are fictional, but not far off in what my meetings generally look like. So, why did I include this boring level of detail in this otherwise extremely fascinating book? Because if your review consists of a cup of coffee, some shiny brochures, and a return figure, then you most likely ain't getting your money's worth!

At least once a year, you should flip the mattress and clean the gutters. Understanding your entire financial picture wouldn't hurt either.

Digging into the Fee Question

Prior to the late 1980s, almost all advisors were commission-based. They put you in something, they got paid. They put you in something else, they got paid again—moving from A to B was how they got compensated. Probably somewhere in the early 1990s, the fee concept started to really grab hold. Some advisors realized people were getting wise to the cost of commissions; the jig was up.

The truth is, the fee concept is better for advisors, many just didn't know it. As advisors, it makes more sense to go fee-based, because it's a steadier income stream. If I'm saying I'm going to charge you 1% a year, I know what that looks like, and you know what that looks like. You also know that when I recommend something, it's not because I'm going to get paid or that my mortgage is due. The more your money grows, the more I'm going to make. So, it's in both our best interests that the money grows; whereas if you're just doing a trade, the advisor doesn't care. He makes his $200 and moves on.

When I first started in 1987, being fee-based really wasn't a thing. I embraced fee-based advising in the late 1990s, yet it wasn't the norm until the last five years. My guess is that many advisors are still at least 30-50% commission-based, but I suspect that will continue to drop in the years to come. To be very clear, someone who is commission-based is not necessarily nefarious. Most of them are very nice people, very well-intended people. That said, human beings are human beings. If a commission-based advisor has two products that are both pretty good for the client, yet one of them pays that advisor 1% and the other one pays 2%, the client is getting the one that pays 2%. Everybody's going to do that, assuming that one product isn't considerably devious compared to the other. So, human nature dictates that this is probably a biased way to deal with clients, versus a fee-based person who is agnostic.

As a fee advisor, the only thing material to my compensation is that the account grows.

Fee-based isn't perfect. There are flaws with fee-based, too, like inactivity. For example, if you had an advisor who was charging you one percent and put you in ten stocks and never did anything again, yet they're still charging you one percent ten years later, you might say, "Well, what the hell are you really doing to earn that fee?" Fair question. The answer may be "a lot." If so, it would make sense to understand the details of "a lot!"

Value Beyond the Initial Transaction

I provide an ongoing service. I meet with my clients usually every quarter, providing them insurance reviews, and guidance on whether they are saving enough. Are they saving in the right places? If they have a 401(k) that's not here, I'm reviewing that. I'm talking to them about estate planning, I'm going to their estate planning meeting with their attorney, yada yada yada. I'm conscious of the fact that in money management, the asset allocation portion of the puzzle is important and ongoing. But if that's all I'm doing for somebody, that's not a lot of value beyond the initial transaction.

I'm very conscious that this team I've built here provides ongoing value to my clients. There's value in things most people take for granted. When you walked in, someone's taking care of you, that person's getting paid. You had a chair to sit in, a water to drink. You need a form? Linda's going to get you the form. You're not going to get it emailed from someone you've never met before, and you're not even sure it's even the right form. You know if you need to talk to me about whether or not to defer your Social Security, I'll be here. What is all of that worth? No one really knows, because it's not really a *thing* that I gave you.

I am making an argument to work with a fee-based advisor. However, where it becomes tough is at the lower end of the marketplace. If you're, say, 26 years old, you don't have $100,000. You may not even have $10,000. And that's the issue with the new Department of Labor law about being a fiduciary. The firms are arguing, "you're going to cut these small people out." They're not going to get advice because nobody gets paid to take care of them. If you say to an advisor: you can't charge this woman and her 25-year-old husband for an A-share mutual (upfront commission) fund, they'll ask, "How am I going to get paid?" Because this couple isn't going to write the advisor a check for $1,000, probably.

The challenge is: the commission-based structure is how young people buy advice. Historically, they'd buy a mutual fund, and the mutual fund company would compensate the advisor. I would argue that we're going to migrate to a better way to handle this. What I mean is that it might be a situation where it's a hybrid robo-set up where the consumer inputs all of their data, and pays $30 a month, or some amount that is reasonable, and they do get an element of human advice along the way as well. Currently we don't have a great platform for this, but I suspect it is right around the corner.

So, is this where the industry is going to go? A service fee, with an affordable and comprehensive process? I hope so. This is a good situation because the advisor doesn't *need* to sell you this or that to make money. The 50-50 split between fee-based advisors and commission-based advisors is going to change. It has to change because it's being mandated by law to change. In Europe, they went through a similar upheaval in their industry and somewhere in the neighborhood of 60% of the advisors got out of the business—because they got rid of commissions.

I believe most folks understand advisors get paid; I just think they would like to know what and how. Crazy, right?

Understand the Two or Three Layers of Costs

People so misunderstand what they're paying now. You should require even your fee-based advisor to show you the cost of the products they're putting you in—to drill down, because they have the tools now to do so. Even though I'm fee-based, I have to put the money somewhere. In my case, it's generally stocks or exchange-traded funds (ETFs), so it's relatively inexpensive, but you need to see that as well.
There's not one layer of fees. There are two or three, many times. I'm often in a competitive situation where I'll go in and talk to a small foundation, for example, and they'll say, "So-and-so showed us this, and it is just stocks." I'll explain, "No, it's not just stocks. Somebody's managing that money." It's called a Separate Account—a glorified mutual fund. "The advisor who showed you

this is not managing the money," I will add. "The advisor is subcontracting that work to some company through their company, and that's not bad. But you need to know there are two layers of costs."

Listen up: it pays (literally) to ask for ALL of the costs. The crazy part is, many advisors don't know ALL of the costs. The advisor is getting paid to service the account, and then somebody's getting paid to manage the account. Then, in the account are ETFs or mutual funds as well, which are managed. Add it up, that's three layers—which ain't always bad, but not knowing usually is.

Going forward, I think you will find that advisors like me are doing both. They have taken back the third-party cost to split between the client and the advisor. It's a win-win for the folks in the trenches—again, the client and the advisor.

Is Your Advisor Keeping Up with The Fire Hose of Change?

On average, I am invited to four or five investment conferences per year, put on by various firms and generally touting a guru or two planning to enlighten me on their brilliance and, more importantly, how to share their brilliance in the form of financial products with my clients. In all fairness, I do go to a few of these each year and, on occasion, even find an event worth both my time and attention.

No matter your industry, you can relate to long meetings in overly cold hotel conference rooms and the tedium that is the corporate educational process.

I've Never Made Anyone Rich

After 37 years, I am still amazed at the number of so-called "Investment Advisors" who are not paying attention to the speakers at all. Let me see if I have this straight? You flew for three hours to hear about ideas that may help your clients, but you have decided that the *USA Today* sports page is a better way to pass the time until tonight's steak dinner? I'm not saying I'm the next coming of Warren Buffett (Jimmy Buffett, maybe), but I do work hard at learning new ideas and hearing what the latest concepts and investment theories are so as to potentially help my clients stay in front of the perpetual threat of bad returns.

I can tell you that while there are many hard working and quite thoughtful financial professionals out there, there are more who are, quite frankly, all about the steak dinner. That's a problem, because my business—and more importantly, the markets you invest in—are constantly changing. Yesterday's good ideas are often tomorrow's gigantic mistakes. If your advisor is not trying to get better, he or she is getting worse.

Make sure your advisor is not only providing you a thoughtful approach and process, but that they are spending time re-educating themselves and keeping you from stagnating in processes and, worse yet, products long past efficacy.

There was a time, for example, that super expensive annuities were all the rage. These products, while far from nefarious, did carry high costs and in return provided investors with guarantees—which often went unused. Today, to my surprise, ten years later those products are still the go-to for many advisors in the retiree market. I'm sure the high commissions have nothing to do with it.

Before annuities, it was limited partnerships. If you were investing in the early 80s you no doubt either bought or at the very least were pitched on one of these gems. More often than not, these "cutting edge" opportunities turned into paper cuts with a nice dash of lemon juice to go with it. (*Princes Bride* people...come on). In short, advisors live in an ever-changing world, and today's brilliance is often tomorrow's Ford Edsel or, for you children of the 80s, AMC Pacer. Remember that interesting car design? Advisors must educate and re-educate quickly or you may end up driving a Pacer.

A logical question right now would be: how would I know if my person is keeping up with the fire hose of change that seems to be the economy and the markets? Good question. Ask 'em! We try our best to share our latest educational endeavors with our clients through email or newsletter, and I promise you that if your person is worth a hoot, she will be happy to do the same.

This year alone, I will travel to three major events and log several thousand miles in the air to do so. It's important that your advisor educates themselves in the right environment. The wrong environment includes events thrown by mutual fund companies and annuity companies. These events can be helpful, but you'll be shocked to find out that they tend to educate on the value of the products they are selling—surprising, I know.

I recommend my advisors attend events put on by analysts and think tanks unaffiliated with any product distributor. I've been to the Wharton School and events put on by major data houses like Dorsey Wright and Morningstar. While not without bias, these tend to be more focused on process over product.
Can you imagine a doctor still using leeches for infection or a dentist still using whiskey as anesthesia? You get the point. Make sure your person stays up to date and is not just in it for the steak dinner.

Is Your Advisor Ethical? Or, Why Did He Offer You That Particular Product?

In this industry, there's an animal called a wholesaler. Wholesalers are people who pitch financial advisors on products they'd like us to pitch to you. They'll take advisors to lunch, dinner, whatever. "We want you to sell your clients this fund. It's awesome, and here's why it's awesome," says the 25-year-old kid who just started last week, full of confidence. That's not necessarily nefarious, but that goes on at levels you can't even imagine to this day.

With a lot of advisors in this business, you own what you own because that one guy took another guy golfing. You should ask, "What are the ethical conundrums, what are the conflicts you have as an advisor?"

For me, a good rule of thumb, just to give one perspective, is an advisor can accept support, or a golf or a fishing trip or whatever, but the advisor may *only do so* if that advisor is *already using* the company offering the support. To be fair, some of these outings are good for mind clearing and information gathering, but should not be the impetus for selling something to a client.

So, the wholesalers don't get to buy a lunch, they don't get to do anything, unless we as a group have *already decided* we want to use this product, not for the reasons the 25-year-old told us, but because it fits with what we're doing. In that case, yes, you can support us because it costs money to retain clients, it costs money to keep clients happy. If we do an event you can support that event because our clients already own the thing. They're not going to buy the thing *because* you supported the event. Therefore, you can support it. It's still not perfect, but those are the realities of the business. Things cost money.

Firms, the big ones, the names you know, must do continuing education events for their advisors and these are supported by the product companies. Again, it's not necessarily a bad or evil thing, because there's a lot of good that comes from those events. We learn a lot about products, about stocks, about analytical tools, about software—a lot of the things I use to provide service to my clients, I learn about at these events. That said, it's something people should understand. They should understand that the pay-for-play still exists in many places.

What Happens to Wholesalers When Commissions Go Away?

I hate to say this because I have a lot of friends who are wholesalers, my contemporaries, guys I've been dealing with for 30 years. I consider them professionals, and consider them valuable; they are great partners in many ways. I don't think they're all going to go away, but I think their compensation is going to change. I think the profession is going to be greatly diminished. The days of the 25-year-old rolling up in a Porsche making $600,000 a year to have lunch is going away. As well it should.

Imagine a doctor, a middle-aged male doctor, prescribing a drug because some attractive 26-year-old female drug rep bought him and his staff ribs from Chili's...wait, that does happen. You get the point.

Does Your Advisor Use the Tools at Their Disposal?

It's not like we have something somebody else doesn't have when it comes to software. But it's the willingness to put in the effort that matters. Advisors are human beings. They want to go have fun with their families, and they want to play golf just like you do. But you need somebody who is willing to take these many tools that we have and use them. You need someone who's willing to put in the time and effort to get you where you need to go. You need someone to have the "whatever it takes" attitude. Investing is a full contact sport; you need a person who's willing to lead and take a hit.

Candidly, most advisors don't crack open the reports available to them nearly as much as I'd like. In addition to advising my clients these past 30 years, I've also had the privilege of being a manager for a good portion of that. This management position allows me to see what other advisors do and do not do. I can see what reports they've run, and how often they're looking at client accounts. I can see those things. Sometimes, I'm disappointed. You should hold your advisor accountable to a review process. With today's technology, an advisor can review and make recommendations to an account or process in a third of the time it used to take. There is no excuse for the advisor to be only looking at your account once a year five minutes before you walk in. Demand excellence; it will make both you and your advisor better.

Are You Gripping Too Tight?

So yeah, I get around. No, you scandalous "Real Housewives"-watching ne'er do wells. Not *that* way. I figured out the other day (without my fingers and toes, mind you) that in my career I have sat down over 15,000 times with clients and/or prospective clients to discuss their finances.

I'm tempted to say I know it all. Problem is, I still don't.

You would think after that many conversations with that many people, I have heard it all. Nope. It seems like once or twice a week someone presents an issue that is either altogether unique or at least in some way different from one I've dealt with in the past.

Facts are, you crazy people each have your own story to tell. Each one of you thinks about money in a different way than the other. Sure, some things are common to each of you. Many will largely under-save and overemphasize things they have no control of. That is common to most of you, some worse than others. Yet each of you has life experiences that you are bound to, and each has your own tolerance for stress.

One thing I'm good at (there's gotta be more than one, right?) is knowing how folks will likely react emotionally to stress, and in particular, to stress associated with money. I can tell usually within an hour of meeting someone who's gonna hang on too tight to the club. For golfers, we know that we should have a loose grip in order for the club head to release and push through the golf ball. If we hold on too tight, the club will, of course, not release and that's how windows get broken and golf clubs thrown. (You know who you are.)

Basically, the one thing I have learned from those 15,000 meetings is who is gripping too tight. I can see it a mile away:

"Scott, what's going to happen with the economy, should we get out or stay in?"

"Should we get some out and keep some in?"

"Should we bury our money out in the backyard or build a bunker for the coming apocalypse?"

"I hear Apple is good...but of course, Steve Jobs is not there anymore. How 'bout Microsoft? My cousin thinks that's a good one. Netflix?"

"Amazon, yeah. They don't make any money, but they do have drones."

Crash, boom, bang...SPLASH! That's your metaphoric golf club landing in the water. Oh, those poor people. It's hard on them. They want to take the risk out of a risky decision. They want to earn 20% without any potential hiccups, not realizing the hiccups most likely are what earn them the return—if they just hold their breath and let them pass. They believe if they just think hard enough and/or read the right publication, "they" will unlock the mystery that is financial success.

Many never change and those folks do not suffer me (the fool) for long, as I will not stop telling them to relax and let the club do the work. To be clear, 15,000 meetings have not yet taught me how to predict the day-to-day gyrations of capital markets.

What it has taught me is who's gonna need a new set of clubs every few months.

Work with a Professional, Not a Yard Sign

The recent increase in signs guaranteeing really good returns on your IRA, like 8%, has led to an interesting phenomenon we'll call Yard Sign Gurus. I find it amazing that in my business, which is amongst the most highly regulated, any yahoo can stick a sign in the ground and claim anything they want. Worse yet, someone must be calling these knuckleheads.

I mean, seriously, as I type this, teams of overpaid analysts, bankers, and ridiculously smart people from schools that wouldn't even let me on campus to empty garbage cans (the list is long) are working feverishly to try and figure out how to get a point or two out in front of the ten-year treasury, which now sits somewhere between 2.5% and doodly-squat.

Yet some think, in their infinite wisdom, "You know, I bet the guy who spent $11.99 on this sign he stuck on the corner is the answer to my money management issues, and while I'm at it, yes, I *would* like to lose 20 pounds in a week without exercise!"

To quote the great Chris Berman, "Come *on,* man!"

The sign I saw today at the street corner asked a simple question: "Would you (yes, you) like to earn 8% on your IRA?"

Now, I'm sure most of you a few years ago would have said yes. In fact, *heck* (or something similar) *yes!* One of the many problems our sign-making financial guru did not consider, however, was that the S&P 500, which is the proxy of most of our market-based investments, earned double digits in 2017. I'm sure once this has dawned on our friend and marketing genius, he will of course catch up with the times and offer you 12%, which is well within the abilities of such a strategist. Okay, why the rant?

The sign just struck me as odd. I mean, do any of you call the numbers on these signs? Does anyone really give their hard-earned money to someone whose credibility is tied up in a sign made from flimsy wire and coated cardboard, and illustrated with a Sharpie? Making a rash decision in hopes of fixing the last decade of pain in one fell swoop based on a slimy guarantee, and the promise of whoever is on the other end of that phone call is probably not the answer.

Key Chapter 9 Takeaways:

- Understand the difference between a fee-based and a commission-based advisor.
- Understand layers of costs and why your advisor wants to put you in a certain product.
- Work with a professional and be willing to pay for their expertise.
- Don't be afraid to ask questions.
- ASK QUESTIONS.
- Be sure your meetings with your advisor cover more than just shiny brochures and impressive return figures. Get into the details with your advisor, and if he or she isn't interested, find someone who is.
- Find out if your advisors are constantly re-educating themselves.
- Know that you cannot take the risk out of a risk decision.

Chapter 10
Products and Buzzwords

The main purpose of the stock market is to make fools of as many men as possible. ~Bernard Baruch

401(k)s: Because You Can't Retire on Complaints

The thing about the 401(k) that drives me crazy is the article a month about 401(k) fees. Annual fees on retirement plans used to be 4%, now they're less than 1%. How much cheaper is it going to get? If it gets much cheaper, no one's going to do it, so there will be fewer providers and thus no competition. It is maddening that the very institution (Congress) that built the 401(k) and mandated its use is the very institution now ridiculing the industry it created. In short, *you're the idiots who created it.* We're just doing what you told us to do, and the funny part is the 401(k) is, hands down, the best way to save for retirement. Where else can you put a dollar in and someone's going to put a dollar on top of it? Okay, sure, it's got fees and the paperwork is sloppy, and maybe sometimes the market sucks. Still, you earn 100% on your money in some cases! The second you put it in your account!

Then, people try to villainize the employers: "They're not paying enough attention, so let's sue them!" So...you're suing the people who gave you free money, basically? There is literally no better way to save for retirement. Now, when you come up with a better way, then you can criticize the crap out of it, *but you don't have one.* We have Social Security, and we see how that's working out. And pensions are done, they're going the way of the Dodo bird.
What you're telling people is, "Here's an excuse not to save for your retirement. The fees are too high, the returns suck, the

advisors and your employers are taking advantage of you!" Well, for some people, that's all they need to hear. Half of all Americans are thinking, "I'm not saving. They're not tricking me!"

This is all to say, I go into this conversation knowing that the 401(k) is the subject of much maligning these days. The gripe by many is that the plans often underperform (subject to opinion) and are overpriced (that, I get). Many believe 401(k)s should be free and earn a substantial guaranteed return—does that sum it up?

Now, before you get all pumped up and start looking for my email address, I, like many of you, believe the 401(k) does have some warts: some fees are still a bit high, and its biggest flaw is that most participants are undereducated and subsequently under-saving. I mean, sure, the plans have their flaws, but I defy you to find me a better place right now to save for retirement.

Go on, I'll wait.

The 401(k) can allow for pre-tax deductions or ROTH after-tax contributions in addition to the fact that most plans have matching contributions from the employer, which, in some cases, can enhance the potential return on every dollar initially invested. Sure, the markets can be difficult, but in my experience, those who put their heads down and keep saving seem more likely to reach their objectives, especially when compared with those who do not save.

Simply put, stop with the excuses and start with the savings. With some regularity, I am approached after a 401(k) enrollment meeting by someone who is, to say the least, annoyed. More precisely, annoyed at me. *Me?* The guy who bought the chicken biscuits for breakfast, *really?* Anyway, this guy (and yes, it's usually a guy) wants me to know the plan sucks! The fees are too high and the returns are terrible! Well now, those are some serious accusations there, big guy. (PS: The diamond earring is really not a great look for a 56-year-old.) I digress.

In most cases, I ask the gentleman if we can meet and look at his account together to see if we can remedy some, if not all, of his concerns. My best guess is that I am taken up on this offer one out of four times. Most folks who complain the loudest are overwhelmed and usually don't know the facts. Those are the semi-thoughtful ones. The one out of four who *do* accept my invitation usually have less than $10,000.00 saved for retirement.

So, let's review. You are 56 years old and have $5,000 saved for retirement and you think the reason for your downfall is high fees and low returns. I got news for you, Einstein. If I double your account this year and reduce your fees to ZERO, you're still screwed. Put some effort into shutting your pie hole and start saving, and then I will be all ears. Otherwise, you're spitting into the wind and I don't intend on getting wet.

Sitting right next to Angry Guy is an older lady who has yet to look up at my presentation and who has properly planned using that same "rotten" plan. She's headed for a secure and comfortable retirement—and that is not fiction. It is easier to be a cynic than to admit saving for retirement is hard. It's easier to gripe about your bad genetics than get up off the couch and hit the gym. It is easier to say the game is rigged than to put in the work to be successful, no matter the endeavor.

In the end, few if any investment platforms are perfect and they all have costs. If they did not, no one would offer them! All that said, you can sit around and complain about it, or you can get on with what you know needs to be done. Because in the end, you can't retire on complaints even if they are free.

A Short History of the 401(k) Plan

The dominant source of retirement savings for most Americans, the 401(k) was invented by a benefits consultant named Ted Benna. It all began in 1978 when Congress decided to alter the tax code with the Revenue Act, and Benna saw the change in the law as an opportunity for employers to create a tax-advantaged savings account for their employees. This type of account or fund is named for a section of the tax code, which went into effect in 1980.

It wasn't designed to be a primary retirement tool. Unlike defined pensions, 401(k) accounts rise and fall with financial markets. Nevertheless, these plans grew in popularity very quickly—by 1983, almost half of large firms considered offering a 401(k). Today, these plans hold $4.8 trillion in assets, and companies are shedding defined pension liabilities as fast as they can.

There are myriad rules and potential loopholes in 401(k)s, but the main ones are as follows. Once you reach age 59 1/2, you can withdraw money from your 401(k) without paying the 10% federal penalty tax, but if you're still working, you'll need to check with your plan administrator. When you reach age 70 1/2, you are required to start taking minimum distributions from your retirement plans, including your traditional IRA and your 401(k).[7] In short, this ain't short term dough, and the IRS wants their pound of flesh before you croak.

---

[7] https://www.cnbc.com/2017/01/04/a-brief-history-of-the-401k-which-changed-how-americans-retire.html and https://www.ebri.org/pdf/publications/facts/0205fact.a.pdf and https://www.sapling.com/8750582/tax-401k-withdrawls-after-65 (Accessed Nov. 25, 2017)

Required Minimum Distributions

Every retirement account lives somewhere, whether it's a bank or a brokerage, and they'll have a custodian who handles the distributions. In our case, every October, my assistant has a list of who is turning 70 ½ the next year, and that calculation is done for them. As an individual investor, if you didn't work with an advisor, it would be incumbent on you to figure out your distribution yourself.

The government theoretically wants your 401(k) depleted by the time you're dead, so they can make their money—the taxes you pay on the disbursements. That 70 ½ rule is based on a mortality table. The good news is recent legislation has been proposed that would extend your RMD to age 72.

Educate or Fail

Often, an employer will opt for the cheapest plan they can find. Usually this is the result of years of media and regulatory pressure put on employers. Employers have basically been beaten into submission by this pressure, so they think they have to make their 401(k) plan cheap at all costs. At least, that's often the perception. If your employer decides to get a low-cost fund with zero education capabilities—a fund that can't educate its participants because it's so cheap, that's not necessarily good. Now you have no participation in your low-cost fund. The number one thing that makes a 401(k) fund successful or not is, in my experience, the owner's willingness to educate.

There's a story in my neck of the woods about two organizations. One of them has about $45 million in assets and a 95% participation rate in its 401(k); the other one has about $16, 17 million in assets and only about a 60 to 70% participation rate. Their participants are far less prepared, on average, to retire. In fact, the average balance in plan one is 20% higher than in plan two. The latter is a much cheaper product whose advisors do next to nothing in terms of education because they're not paid to do it. Cost is all they care about. The first organization I mentioned is all about education and ongoing events, and contributes mightily to get people involved. I think you see the difference in outcomes. Once again, you cannot discount your way to success.

IRAs

When I used to explain IRAs, Individual Retirement Accounts, to people back in the day, they would always ask, "How does your IRA do?" Well, that's a hard question to answer. An IRA is not an investment, an IRA is a bucket. Whatever you put in that bucket is tax deferred and tax deductible, but it's just a bucket. So, you can put a CD in your bucket, you can put a mutual fund in your bucket, you can put a stock in your bucket, you can put a bond in your bucket. All those things earn different rates of return. The IRA is just a tax law, a set of rules, and whatever you put in there gets the favorable tax treatment.

People think an IRA is a product, just as some people think a 401(k) is a product: "My 401(k) is awesome!" Is your 401(k) awesome, or is the stock market up 20%, which is why you *think* your 401(k) is awesome?

People get a little confused about traditional IRAs versus ROTH IRAs. The thinking behind a traditional IRA is whatever you put into it each year would be deducted from your taxable income. You would then pay taxes on that money during your retirement years, when your rate is lower. People used to think the discrepancy made that worthwhile. The problem is, I don't know how true that is anymore. If you're a person of means now, you'll still be a person of means in retirement. You're not going to go from $100,000 in income each year to $10,000 in income. You might go to $80,000, which means your tax rate isn't going to change that much. So, the argument is simply, do you pay taxes now, or do you pay them later?

I would argue, for anybody over 50, there's not enough time to offset the immediate value of the tax deduction. Meaning if you're older, you probably shouldn't be putting much of your money in a ROTH. If you're under 40, I think ROTH is a no brainer. It's a matter of how long your money has to grow, and no two situations are the same. I'm often irritated (yes, I'm easily irritated) when someone tells me, "So-and-so says ROTHs are bad." *ROTHs are bad?* What the hell does that mean? ROTHs may or may not be optimal for some folks, but they are neither good nor bad.

Gravity

John Mayer says it's working against me.

Gravity is a funny thing, especially as you get older. Am I right or am I right? Let's just say gravity ain't no good for the human body as time marches on. Stuff isn't where it used to be, and where it used to be is where I/we want it.

Kind of like your 401(k). What?! I know, stay with me here. When you are working and diligently saving in your 401(k), it seems to always move forward. Sure, sometimes the amount it grows is minimal in any given year and sometimes it's flat, but it seems, at least, to always do okay. For example, in a bad year a 401(k) with $50,000.00 in it might experience a 5% drop due to market conditions, but because you and your company are adding to it, your balance shows higher at year's end. More dramatically, if an account rises by 5% or $2,500.00, and you add an equal or greater amount, the year-end balance looks considerably more fantastic than it actually should.

But when you retire, gravity becomes just as much a factor on your old 401(k) as it does on your eyelids. Most people, upon retiring, have a hard time understanding the dramatic effect gravity (withdrawals) has on a portfolio, especially when blindly (see what I did there) comparing outcomes to their days of saving in the same account. When you add to an account, the sequence of your returns is really unimportant as long as the returns eventually come. Conversely, taking a monthly withdrawal from your account now has the opposite effect on your balance than the contribution once did, in that it makes a decent year look mediocre and a bad year look catastrophic.

As an example, let's say you and your advisor agree to withdraw 4% per year from your capital. You both think this is a reasonable amount, and based on historical research, you move forward. In your first year, you make 6% and find your, let's say $100,000.00 account is only up $2,000.00. You feel okay, yet somehow disappointed to see your balance stagnate in a decent market year.

Even more extreme is the year the market drops 5%. It doesn't seem like a terrible year, but when you add your 4% or $4,000.00 withdrawal to our hypothetical $100,000, you find yourself not only down the $4,000 but an additional $5,000 for a total drop of $9,000.00. If you harken back to your days of contributing, you may not have even noticed a decline of 5% in your 401(k), but today it feels terrible.

Worse yet, your balance, as a result of the withdrawal and market drop, has been reduced to $91,000.00. Why is that bad? Well, if you continue to take $4,000.00 per year now on $91,000.00 instead of $100,000.00, your formerly reasonable withdrawal of 4% has become a not-as-reasonable withdrawal of 4.4% and, while not a historically crazy number, not what you had in mind.

Great, you're thinking. *What's a person to do to avoid this "gravity" you speak of?*

For starters, every retiree should keep at least a year's cash on hand to supplement their incomes should markets turn south. This can help avoid the need to sell securities in a downturn, which compounds the issue. Secondly, that cash should come from the account when returns are in excess of expected withdrawals. When you make it, stash it. When things aren't so rosy, use that stash to help keep the account firm and sexy. This is Scott's law of disproportionate returns. You're welcome.

Annuities Killed My Grandfather

Annuities elicit such a dramatic response one way or another. My dad hated annuities! Annuities killed my grandfather! Okay, that's a bit extreme...annuities rarely kill people.

An annuity is a tool, no different than a hammer. You can drive the hell out of a nail with a hammer, but you can't wash a window very well. If you view annuities as evil or good, you're missing the point. They're neither. It's how you use them.

There are several types of annuities. The first type that people are more commonly familiar with now are variable annuities. Variable annuities are wrappers that insurance companies create with benefits that have mutual funds, or an investment component. So, you put a dollar into an annuity, and somewhere in the neighborhood of three or four cents are going to go to costs that pay for benefits. That's the point of having the insurance wrapper. Those benefits could include, but are not limited to, a death benefit. In some examples, you could put $100,000 in a variable annuity, and they say, look, as long you don't withdraw anything, it doesn't matter what the market does. If the market goes up 30% and the value of your account is up $30%, great. You die, your heirs will get $130,000. But, what we're going to do for you for the three or four percent you're paying us, is if the market goes down to $80,000 and you die, your heirs are going to get $100,000. We're going to make them whole. There's value in that. How much? I'm not sure.

If you say, *I don't need that money, I'm going to shoot for the moon, I'm just leaving it to my kids*, maybe that's not a bad strategy and worth paying for.

Conversely, if you put the money in the mutual fund or a stock, and the market goes to 80, your heirs get $80,000. They don't get $100,000. Is getting rid of that risk worth paying for? That's up to each individual. There are also living benefits sometimes, which may say something like, if you give us $100,000, we're going to guarantee to pay you 5% of that $100k for the rest of your life, regardless of what the market does.

An example of someone who might need that is an unsophisticated investor who worked in a blue-collar industry and ended up with a nice pension. They might've come away with $500,000, which is not an insignificant amount of money. They might say, "Listen, we don't really understand this stuff, but we need $25,000 a year. My wife and I must have that." There is no vagary here. So, we say, "Okay, you could put that in mutual funds, you could put that in bonds to produce $25,000 a year. But...if the market comes unglued, then that would not be the case." Versus an annuity where you're going to pay more on an annual basis, but they're promising you as long as John Hancock is still in business, they're going to pay you your $25k, even if that $500k turns into $200k. The husband might say, "If I die, I need my wife to still get that money." So, that certainty is part of what you're paying for.

Somebody else might say, "For 1%, I'm willing to take the risk that the market is going to go up and down, but I'm already 2% ahead of the game." So, there's no right or wrong answer. Do not get married to absolutes. Absolutes are usually anything but. Think, people!

Once Suze Orman was on TV and she was saying, "Annuities are the worst thing in the world!" Okay, it's kind of a blanket statement. Someone calls in and says, "My husband bought us an annuity back in 1995, we put in $400,000 and the market fell apart, and it dropped to $300,000, and he died, and they gave me $400,000. Suze, what was wrong with that?"

She stammered and stuttered, because clearly that was an example of when it made sense and it actually worked. It did what it was supposed to do. If she had had that money in stocks, she would've only gotten $300,000. Suze struggled because she had made such a blanket statement. I can't remember what she said, but it was clear she was uncomfortable, or maybe it was just the leather pants she was wearing?

Another example is the fixed annuity, something called an immediate annuity. This is really how the whole business got started back in the 70s.

If you come to me and you say, "Scott, I am 75 years old, and I have $200,000 and I need $16,000 a year." I'll say to you, "Well, that's 8%, that's not going to happen. But, if you give me the $200,000, I'll give it to XYZ insurance company and they'll give you the $16,000 a year. They're guaranteeing the income, but it's not your money now. They've run the mortality table, and they expect you to live this long, and if you don't live that long, they win. So that's the chance they'll take to give you the 8% versus the 3% the market's paying right now, but you have to give up the capital."

For some people, this is a must. That's their only option. Is it an awesome option, because they don't have the $200k anymore? No...but if all other things are being considered, and they *have to have* the $16,000? That's what they do. It's not something I would tend to advise anyone to do. I've probably only done this kind of transaction five times in 30 years because this was the exact situation.

Most people would say, "That's awful! You gave up your $200,000! What were you thinking?" But if that person lives 20 more years, then it was a pretty good thing. If they outlive the mortality table they win...if not, well, they're dead, so it's likely they won't care.

Annuities are not good or bad, they're just tools.

Insure It

I'm not an insurance expert by any stretch, but insurance is a necessary evil. We all hate it, we all hate paying for it, yet health insurance is necessary. Life insurance, depending on the circumstance, can be necessary. I think the thing that people need to understand about insurance, especially all the life insurances being peddled out there, is as a young family in your twenties, you could probably buy permanent whole life insurance for a hundred bucks a month or less, and then you'll have it forever. Whether you get sick, diabetes, whatever, they can't take it from you. There's value in doing that if you can afford it.

I think while you have a family, you need some form of insurance.

My uncle hated insurance. He didn't want to ever buy it, it's a scam, et cetera. Well, it's a scam for *him*, because he'd be dead. But what about the kids at home who still need to eat? I always thought it was very selfish of him. The truth was, I think he hated giving blood and didn't want to do the physical, if I were to guess. He's still alive, and I love him, but that was less than cool in my book and a little selfish, looking back.

If you have children, if you're the breadwinner, you have a responsibility to this person you created, and to your significant other, who's going to be stuck holding the bag if you croak. I do believe insurance is important.

I don't agree with people who, later in life, are still paying $10k for certain insurances when their kids have flown the coop, and they have significant assets. Until they get into an estate planning issue, until they get into a situation where now they have $30 million, they probably don't need to pay exorbitant insurance premiums. You may have tax issues, depending on the current administration's success or lack thereof. Taxes are high when you leave money beyond the estate tax threshold. So, I do think there's some value in insurance even if you have considerable means, but most of us are not going to be in that category.

When You Get Your Colonoscopy, We'll Talk about Long-Term Care Insurance

Long-term care insurance is becoming more and more important. We're living longer, we're often requiring care that's very expensive. I didn't want to sell it in the past, because it was an uncomfortable conversation with people. When it first came out, it was *use it or lose it*. Many people had policies where they were paying $5,000 a year, and never went into a facility. They were like, "what the hell was I paying for?" But insurance products have evolved; now they may have death benefits and cash values in them. Are they great investments? No. Are they great uses of money for long-term care? Yes. You can use more of the hybrid products that are available.

I'm seeing it in my own clients. As I'm aging, I'm seeing clients who get $10k of care paid for each month by insurance companies, and I'm seeing people who don't have it watching $10k of their estate go out the door each month until they're completely broke. I would bring up long-term care insurance with a client at age 50. When you get your colonoscopy, we'll talk about long-term care insurance. It's such a pleasant week or two for you!

When it comes to life insurance, the industry sees about 60 to 70 percent persistency, which means for every ten people who buy life insurance around seven of them keep paying for the term of the policy. In long term care insurance, it's over 90 percent. Because people realize, *holy shit, I'm going to need this.* My wife plays tennis with a bunch of middle-aged women, and the stories continue to come in: "My mom went in, she broke a hip," or "My dad has dementia and keeps lighting his cigar with a blowtorch near the curtains." It's funny, but not really. Those stories always end one of two ways: "Thank god for the insurance check every month" or, "How are we going to pay for this?" and, "So much for the inheritance."

I'm more on it now as an advisor than I used to be. I'm still reluctant, because it's an insurance conversation and I don't, honestly, love those conversations. People see it as used car sales-y, and I don't like that feeling. But that's my hang-up and I need to get past it to recognize that as a planner, this is a vital part of the whole picture.

HSAs

Health Savings Accounts are a simple tool that allows account owners to pay for current health care expenses and save for those that might arise in the future, tax-free. Right now, more and more Americans are becoming eligible for HSAs because high deductible health insurance plans are more common. You can only have an HSA if you have a high deductible plan.

What's so great about HSAs? First, contributions are tax-deductible. If they are made through a payroll deduction, they are pre-tax. This means you lower your taxable income for the year when you contribute to an HSA account. Second, interest earned on your account is all tax-free, and the account isn't tied to a particular job. Finally, account owners may make tax-free withdrawals at any time for qualified medical expenses.

For those who want to save for the future, your tax liability is reduced with an HSA. If you grow your HSA and accumulate a balance into retirement, after you reach the age of 65 you can use the money tax-free on qualified medical, vision and dental expenses not covered by Medicare. Or, you can withdraw the balance to use for other purchases and pay income taxes much like a 401(k).

The tax advantages of HSAs are good for those who have high deductible health insurance plans. Again, with an HSA, owners can make pre-tax contributions, earn tax-free interest, and make tax-free withdrawals. Anyone willing to spend some time learning about HSAs can benefit from the tax savings.

Mutual Funds and ETFs, Exchange Traded Funds

There are mutual funds that buy stocks, there are mutual funds that buy bonds, there are funds that buy only international stocks, small cap stocks, mid cap stocks, some do it all—they're go anywhere funds. There are mutual funds that short the market. There are mutual funds that buy commodities, silver, gold, oil. There's a mutual fund that does virtually everything. Mutual funds are historically the way the public invests money—whether it's in their 401(k) or not, they're ubiquitous.

That said, they're beginning to lose their luster a bit because of cost—people are more conscious of the cost of mutual funds. There are a million studies out there that say 85% of actively managed mutual funds, which is what they are, actively managed, are going to lose on an annual basis to the index. You hire a fund manager, you pay that person or team 1%, and the S&P 500 beats them most years. So, it's like hiring a doctor every year who continues to not make you better. What is the point of that? Mutual funds are struggling with that identity crisis.

In some very esoteric asset classes, like international or emerging markets, or currency exchanges, or options-based products, or even small cap stocks, a fund manager *can* provide you a level of value, because the research becomes more important in those asset classes. Whereas if you're buying a growth fund, there's just no value in purchasing an actively managed fund in lieu of an index fund. Seriously, why would you pay someone to buy Microsoft and Amazon when you could do it yourself for much cheaper? In our practice we use them, but only for the aforementioned esoteric asset classes.

So, are mutual funds good? Are mutual funds bad? It's just not that simple. Again, it's a tool. How you use that tool, how you manage the costs of that tool, and how you determine its effectiveness must be considered on an individual basis. A good advisor should be able to explain these issues to you. Why are you using a manager *here*, and using an index *here*? I would say most individuals should be doing both.

ETFs, in which you're essentially buying the index, are very popular right now; there seems to be ten of them coming out every day. By and large, ETFs are not actively managed, but even that is changing. ETFs are kind of the rage right now because they are, quote unquote, indexes, thereby less expensive. That's part of the fee compression in the industry. ETFs are starting to make their way into 401(k)s, and there's a lot of discussion around it. *Is that good, is that bad, does that matter? Are boards and companies too focused on costs right now?* If you have a great fund and low fees, yet no one participates in it, that is its own problem, as we discussed previously.

Wall Street money managers are all trying to stop their mutual fund bleeds by coming out with ETFs. So, the wholesaler who sold mutual funds three years ago and hated ETFs now sells ETFs too. The ETF industry, like any industry, wants to make money. As a result, now they're coming up with "Smart ETFs" which are basically mutual funds in disguise that the industry can charge a little bit more for. They might say it's the S&P 500 PLUS some really extra smart stocks that we think are awesome. Whatever.
Having said that, ETFs are a good development for a guy like me who wants to manage money for a smaller investor, let's say a person who has $50,000. Well, I can't buy that person 50 stocks. It's just cost prohibitive for them, it's hard to keep up with, it's unwieldy. But I can buy them an ETF that owns those stocks for 20 basis points, one quarter of one percent, whereas before you would have to had paid one, one and a half percent. It's not perfect, but it's better.

Most advisors get paid to be the middleman, but I think over time more firms will be run like mine is run: we're buying the stocks, we're buying the ETFs, so we've eliminated one layer of cost for you. Mutual funds—they're still the most popular thing. But I think that's going to change within ten years. I think you're going to see a lot of flow out of mutual funds. It's an extra layer of cost. If you come to me and say, "Scott, I'd like to invest," I'm going to say, "Great, I'm going to buy you Exxon, AT&T, Procter & Gamble and Johnson & Johnson," that's one conversation. If I say instead that I'm going to buy the XYZ Growth Fund, now we've got to pay XYZ Growth Fund, in addition to you and me. Understanding that dynamic is important. Now, that's not to say we *shouldn't* pay XYZ Growth Fund for some things, for some expertise. It might be worth it.

It's not all or nothing. As always, there are no absolutes...are you paying attention?

Separately Managed Accounts (SMAs)

You go to your broker and you say, "Hey, is there anything fancier than a mutual fund? Anything sexier than a mutual fund?" Well, your broker might say, "I know the manager down at UBS, and he runs the Joe Blow Fund and I know him! He buys the stocks! Of course, he's only for our special clients." Wink, wink. Don't you feel special now? You shouldn't.

So, is an SMA any different than a mutual fund? The answer is, not really. It's kind of the same thing. The advantages of an SMA are, they would argue, tax efficiency if it's a non-qualified account, meaning it's not an IRA. How does that work? Well, you might be able to call up Joe Blow in the Joe Blow Fund, and say, "Listen, I've got a loss in Procter & Gamble. Can you sell that for me, because tax time is coming? I'll absorb that loss and buy it back in 30 days or whatever." They might be able to do that for you. Whereas you can't call up Fidelity and say, "I want you to sell AT&T." They're going to laugh at you. So, there are some advantages to SMAs. But how often does this scenario happen? Not very often.

It's just a sexier wrapper on the same thing, for the most part. They are, on the whole, less expensive than a mutual fund, but then you have to add the advisor cost back on top of it. If you pay Joe Blow 30 basis points or half a percent, the advisor still wants their one percent.

Alternative Investments (Hedge Funds)

If you tell a wealthy investor they can buy a hedge fund, they get all excited. Honestly, it doesn't mean squat. It's just a different way to say the same thing. A hedge fund could be anything. They could buy real estate, stocks on the exchange, oil futures, a share in Aerosmith. When you call something a hedge fund, you're saying they can do whatever they want, including lose their asses. The list of hedge funds that have had their butts kicked by the S&P this year is long and distinguished.

For that privilege, they're going to charge you twice what an average mutual fund does. More often than not, they're not better than anything else, but it is a sexy thing that firms put together to try to sell to advisors. It's the scarcity thinking again: "Ooh, it's exclusive." It's like putting gates on a community and a guard at the front. Somehow that makes everything worth $100k more. It's all perception.

Socially Responsible Funds—Otherwise Known as the Funds That Struggle to Make Money

To be fair, many of them do fine. But I think the screening process is wildly different from one to another. Alcohol, tobacco, how do you screen for all that stuff? Some conglomerate may own thirty different companies. Or they're doing business with a foreign government that we deem undesirable; well, who determines that? I think being able to see the underbelly of that stuff is hard.

I would argue there's not a single stock you could buy that you could say isn't involved in *something* undesirable. Even Apple.

Somebody could say, "people use Apple products to look at pornography, or people use Apple to do illicit trades," and so on and so forth. I get it, and I appreciate and respect the effort to improve the world in some small way. Sometimes it's just about making an effort, and we all have to decide how much of an effort we want to make. However, at the end of the day, I think a lot of the socially responsible fund thing is marketing smoke and mirrors. If you're trying to save the world, this ain't the way to do it.

The Perfect Investment

In nearly 30 years of dealing with people and their money, one thing seems to remain somewhat constant. If asked, most middle-class Americans will say that the best investment they have ever made is in their homes.

The question is, why? Is it because the average primary residence in America has appreciated considerably more than an investment in, say, the S&P 500 or the bond market? According to the U.S. Census Bureau, new homes have appreciated by 5.4% per year from 1963 to 2008. Conversely, over that same period the stock market, as measured by the S&P 500, earned 9.41%.

In fairness, the bond market over the last ten years has come in around 4.62%, according to thebalance.com, when looking at all bonds in the aggregate. The bottom line here is that real estate, while a good investment, is not considerably better or worse than most other asset classes. So, this begs the question, why do most people believe their home to be the best investment they have ever made?

Well, for starters, they made the investment. When a person makes an investment decision on their own, they will go to the ends of the earth to defend that decision. It's like doctors. We've all had to listen to people who are getting a surgery or procedure done and sharing with you the prowess of said doctor. You know, "This gall bladder doctor is the best in the country. She's so good people who don't have gallbladder problems are having them removed just to be on the business end of her knife!" No one ever says, "I need a triple bypass, but the good surgeon is in Aruba, so I'm having this other guy who generally loses 80% of his patients take a whack at it."

I believe if and when people make mediocre or worse decisions, they are gonna slap as much lipstick as possible on the description as is necessary to validate that decision. Having said all that, is this the main reason people believe their homes are the best investment they've ever made? Nope. The main reason is because they are right. Huh…this is not the outcome I was expecting.

The reason they correctly believe their real primary residence is the best investment they have ever made is because during those periods when its return is not stellar ('07, '08, '09, '10, '11) they CANNOT sell it. I mean they could, but living in a tent or in a van down by the river usually does not sit well with the wife and kids. It's a forced hold, period. End of sentence.

Most people understand that even if their home were to depreciate, as Will Rogers once said, "They don't make any more if it" (real estate) and it is likely that in a few years they will be just fine. If we treated our securities portfolios the same way, the averages tell us that long-term outcomes are likely to be as good as those of our homes. Holding a quality (that's the tricky part, I know) security for 30 years, historically, can provide both income and growth that rewards patience.

Revenge of the Bonds: *The Waiting is the Hardest Part*

As the great philosopher Tom Petty once said, "Most things I worry about never happen anyway."

After several client meetings this month, I realized that many of my clients, and I am sure, many more of you, still don't get the deal with bonds, the Fed, and interest rates. I try really hard to stay away from technical jargon and detailed investment ideas, mainly because I think most issues people have with money stem largely from their inability to apply the common sense they generally have an abundance of to the accumulation of wealth.

That said, I'm going to risk running afoul of the word referees in order to give you some insight into a largely misunderstood group of securities: bonds.

As Will Rogers once said, "It's not return *on* my principal I'm concerned with, it's return *of* my principal I'm concerned with."

Thus, the life of a bond holder.

What is a bond? A bond is basically an I-owe-you issued by a bank, a corporation, a state or city government, or of course, the United States Treasury (we store those in China for safekeeping—I jest). In return for lending the aforementioned group money, they agree to pay us a specific amount of interest. So, for example, the XYZ Company wants to build a new factory. They may issue a ten-year bond that will be purchased by investors for some predetermined amount of interest. We'll say 5% just for fun. Over the course of the ten years we might own this XYZ bond, rates will go up and probably go down.

This is where it gets interesting (I swear).

If rates go up and XYZ has to pay its new creditors 6%, what do you think will happen to the value of your 5% bond? Good answer Mr. Spicoli: your bond will drop in value because, of course, the only way someone would buy a 5% bond in a 6% market is at...you guessed it, a discount.

That brings us to today. Over the last few months, bondholders have seen their bonds, like our ten-year XYZs, drop in value on their statements. Some are wondering if they should sell, largely because they are concerned they might drop further if rates continue to increase. Well, it turns out they are right to worry, but largely wrong to sell, unless, of course, they have an immediate need for the money. If we assume we paid $100.00 for each of our 5% bonds with XYZ and today they trade at $99.00, then our fear might be they will go to $98.00 or worse. The truth is, they might...so what?

Barring a collapse of XYZ and a default, when our bond comes due, it will come due at the $100.00 price we paid for it and we will be made whole. Once again, Tom Petty would have been proven correct. I should mention that bonds have all kinds of risk factors including length of term and the entity's ability to pay.

Bonds may be in for a rough ride these next few months and possibly longer, but if you understand the relationship of your bonds to interest rates, you might avoid a common mistake.

Social Security—When to Begin Taking It

This is a tough one because no one knows when they're going to die. People say, "Can you tell me which is best for me?" and I can't. But think of it this way, if you have longevity on your side, your mother is 103 years old, and you're still playing tennis every day, then delaying is a no brainer, because you're literally earning 8% a year on that income.

Let's say your full retirement age is 66 and you can only push it to 70. If you were going to get Social Security at 66, it was $1500 a month, and if you wait until you're 70, it's $2,000. Well, that's an extra $6,000 a year for the entire rest of your life! I know the market's been doing well, but no one can guarantee you 8%. Yet Social Security is guaranteeing you 8%. So, if you're healthy, you work out, you do all the stuff we're supposed to do, you're not eating cookies all day, then it probably makes sense to delay.

The next question is always, "is it going to be around?" Well, people have been telling me Social Security's going away for thirty years, and certainly there are solvency issues, but I always say this: "Do you want to be the Senator whose district is The Villages, a giant retirement community in Florida, when the checks stop coming?" The answer is, "probably not." So, they're going to figure it out. Are they going to raise the threshold that we have to pay taxes on so that we kick in more to support Social Security? Probably. Nobody wants to be chased by a bunch of geriatrics in golf carts.

When the Committee on Economic Security (CES) proposed age 65 as the retirement age under Social Security in 1935, the number stemmed from a general observation about standard retirement ages in the few private pension systems in existence at the time, and the 30 state-run pension systems then in operation. About half of the state pension systems used age 65 as the retirement age; half used age 70. The new federal Railroad Retirement System also used age 65 as its retirement age. Actuarial studies at the time showed using age 65 produced a manageable system that could easily be made self-sustaining with only modest levels of payroll taxation.[8]

So, when they initially said, "everyone gets Social Security at 65," the average life expectancy was around 64. There's your solvency issue. They didn't expect most of us to get it, and it was never designed to be the sole source of income for anyone. It was designed in the day of pensions, it was designed when people saved money. People get really indignant about Social Security, which I understand—but it ain't as cut and dried as chasing those damn kids off your lawn.

Robo-Advisors

Remember the old TV show *Get Smart?* I'll give you a second. You know, the one where the often-bumbling secret agent Maxwell Smart bounces around the world with the understanding that he is both brilliant, and the primary reason the world has not been taken over by his rival, KAOS.

Ah, the good ole days of TV, rabbit ears, three channels and your little brother standing on one leg while holding a coat hanger next to the set so the picture would not fade. It seems to me that today's financial services model looks a lot like *Get Smart*. In the role of KAOS are the financial markets and the multitude of bad information and attention-grabbing headlines. Combine that with a financial services industry that is bent on selling you a new

---

[8] https://www.ssa.gov/history/age65.html Accessed January 31, 2018.

"better" product every day, and TV ads promising "new" ways to trade your way to riches, and you indeed have a recipe for KAOS.

I mean, if these day trading programs really worked, wouldn't the people "selling" the day trading programs just be, well, *day trading?* Speaking of trading technology, it seems that there is a new robo application coming out every day. Great, now we not only have to deal with markets and Wall Street, but now we must deal with the damn robots?

The concept, as you may or may not know, is that the robos will simply allow you to input your hopes and dreams in the form of personal economic data and sit back and wait for the robo to spit out a miracle formula for your dream financial outcome.

Here's the problem...chaos.

There are two chaos theories. Chaos theory one is best described as weather. We can (sometimes) predict the weather, within reason. Despite our complaints, the meteorologist is usually close. The fact that the weatherperson says it's going to rain will not in any way, shape, or form change the pattern of said weather. It will or will not rain despite what the weatherman says.

Chaos theory two, which applies to "financial algorithms" (robos), goes more like this: I determined that every third Friday the market goes up, and thus I built an algorithm in my robo to buy stocks for my clients on Thursday afternoon. Pleased with my brilliance, I sit back and wait for the money to roll in. And for a while, it might.

I say *for a while* because after a few months of doing this, I start to see that my returns are dropping somewhat precipitously and set about investigating why.

After seeing my success, a few other robos decided to ride my coattails and also began buying on Thursday afternoon. The problem with this is that once more than a few of us figured out the secret formula, the formula changed. The formula of buying on Thursday and profiting on Friday no longer worked because many of us were now paying more on Thursday then we used to, and buying on Friday diminished. Thus, the "Third Friday Algorithm" no longer worked. Type two chaos, when understood, changes itself. In short, we "missed it by that much."

Robos are coming and they will continue to improve and maybe even prove to be useful tools in gathering and keeping track of wealth. However, they are not a good substitute for common sense and long-term, disciplined investing. You cannot plug in some personal data and have a miracle come out the other end without discipline and thoughtful planning.

In other words, this robo-movement is not going to turn out the way people think it's going to turn out. Even with millennials and the younger group—and I don't like bunching them together because I think they're as unique as anybody else—this idea of having everything on your phone is not going away, but I still think human beings, whether they are 14 or 94, crave confirmation from a trusted partner.

I think we'll be able to marry the technology of what we call aggregation in the business—meaning, I can see everybody's accounts on my phone, and they see them on their phone. But most people still want, at the end of the day, a conversation about what's *on* that phone. An investor can't ask the phone, "I was thinking about doing this, do you believe it would be a savvy move?" I mean, you could but I would personally be reluctant to let "Alexa" decide which stock to buy or whether or not covered calls made sense on my biggest stock position.

Here is a classic example of a conversation you can't have with a phone or with a robo-advisor:

I had a client come in the other day, and he was thinking about selling his primary residence and moving into the condo that he had just inherited from his mother. My first thought was, "Your wife's not going to live in the 900-square-foot condo. I know she says she will, but you and I both know she's not going to like that. A. And B, look, I've been doing this for a long time, and here is something I'm sure of. I know you pretty well. You're an okay saver, but not great. You do dumb stuff from time to time. If you rent out that condo, you've already told me you can get rent that will more than cover your mortgage. In short, the renter will pay for your condo over the long term."

His choice was give me a hundred grand to invest, or pay off the house, so I said, "If you give me a hundred grand, I know you have a hundred grand. But if you pay off the mortgage, you're not going to save that hundred grand back up again. You could have one bird in hand, or two birds in hand. At the end of the day, once the house is paid off, you have that asset, and you still have the original $100k plus interest. But if you put it into the house, you'll spend most of the extra money you have floating around each month on nothing. So, let's do what I believe will work for you, a self-imposed discipline." He then took me to the parking lot to see his new Porsche to validate my "you suck at saving" point.

Human knowledge of this person's habits and personality was the key to being able to genuinely help him.

I have other clients whom I would counsel to pay off their houses because I know they're not going to blow the extra money every month after that. I can think of tons of clients who say they're going to pay something off and save the difference, and I'm 100% sure they're going to do that.

He was not one of those people. He readily admitted it. But he needed a human being to remind him.

Robos in 2024

Since the initial publication of this book, several robo offerings have either gone out of business or been acquired by large advisory firms like UBS. Wealthfront and Personal Capital, amongst others, have been gobbled up as their offerings proved less appealing to investors than anticipated.

In the end, "affluent" and "affluence seeking" individuals want and need human input. Robots can't take ideas and build a story. Every investor has an incomplete story in their head that requires another human being to bring to a satisfying and thoughtful end. The story has twists and turns that no code can be written for.

Tax implications, deaths, births, and emotions are part of the story – arguably the only part that matters. There has never been and will never be a formula that includes ones and zeros that can be translated into the oh-so-human experience that is planning one's financial journey. The journey is not simply "math," the journey is an emotional rollercoaster that requires real time interactions with real people feeling real emotions.

These "reals" cannot be anticipated by an algorithm. Robo-type offerings remain a viable tool when interacting with returns, allocations, and meaningful data points. They are not and never will be adequate for calming human beings when things become difficult, nor will they replace human compassion when economics meet the death of a spouse or the birth of a grandchild.

Key Chapter 10 Takeaways:

- Participate in your company's 401(k).
- Don't obsess too much over 401(k) fees.
- The best 401(k) funds are the ones that educate participants.
- There are no inherently evil financial products. They're tools.
- Be aware of gravity, or the compounding effects of withdrawals.
- Be sure you are adequately insured.
- Robo-advisors may have their place in the market, but they cannot and should not do everything.

Chapter 11
Risk

The planning fallacy is that you make a plan, which is usually a best-case scenario. Then you assume that the outcome will follow your plan, even when you should know better.
~Daniel Kahneman

If you won't take risks, the returns just won't be there. If you sit in your house, you probably won't get hurt, you probably won't get run over by a bus, but *damn*, that is a boring way to go through life. There's no reward in that.

I remember the first time I went to Guatemala, I thought, "I don't know what I'm doing, I'm in the middle of the woods." But at some point, I decided if this is how I go out, this is how I go out. And if I don't, what an awesome, new enlightenment I will have.

I no longer view risk as something to avoid. In fact, I view it as an opportunity to take advantage of. The facts are that most Americans abhor risk, and subsequently live a mundane and profitless "risk free" life.

Let's Talk Risk Tolerance. You Have Less of It Than You Think.

When you review your brokerage statements, which most likely reflect last year's performance, my suspicion is that you will first notice the number is decent and then shortly thereafter realize it is not the 20-30% the various stock-based indexes earned recently.

You will then pick up the phone, call your advisor, and demand an explanation as to why this is so. I mean, seriously, if the indexes are up 25% or so, why in the world am I only up 11% or 9%?! Is it too much to ask that you keep up with the indexes...?

YES, it is. Now I'm going to explain why that is not only too much to ask, but why it is shortsighted—and why you don't want your advisor chained to one index or another. For that, your advisor is welcome.

I would be willing to bet that if I had called each of you on January 1, 2019 and offered you a guaranteed 9% or 11%, you would've said YES as fast as you could. Studies have shown over and over again that humans (most of you qualify) anchor their individual happiness or, more precisely their individual success, to the success or perceived success of those around them.

In a study done years ago, psychologists asked a group of suburban homeowners if they would rather live in a neighborhood where they earned $80,000.00 per year and their neighbors earned on average $70,000.00 per year, or in a neighborhood where they earned $90,000.00 per year and their neighbors on average earned $100,000.00 per year.

You guessed it: the former was the choice, hands down, despite the fact that they would earn $10,000.00 less on an annual basis. In a second study, a group of individuals was asked to play a game in which they had a 50% chance of either winning $32.00 or winning $8.00. After playing the game, the PhDs involved asked the participants who had won only $8.00 how they felt and, as you might expect, they were in all cases disappointed. One week later those same folks were asked to participate in a similar game, only this time the two outcomes were limited to losing $32.00 or losing $8.00. Right again, the same people who were disappointed to have won $8.00 weeks earlier were to a person pleased to have lost $8.00.

My point is threefold. First, academics sure do have a lot of time on their hands. Second, very few investors have the risk tolerance to be in a portfolio that is in 100% stocks. If you don't believe me, get into Marty McFly's DeLorean and travel back to 2009 and ask yourself. Third, stop assessing your success by what you perceive your neighbor's (or obnoxious brother-in-law's) success to be. It is this mentality that tends to get us all in trouble. The truth of the matter is that most folks who tell you how great they're doing often leave out their missteps. I have found "most rivers run loudest at their shallowest points."

The Dreaded Risk Questionnaire

I am willing to bet that each and every one of you, or at the very least most of you, have at some point sat down on your own or at the urging of a financial advisor and taken one of those now ubiquitous "risk" questionnaires. I think I heard you all sigh at the same time. The purported purpose of those questionnaires is to assess what your tolerance for market volatility is.

The real purpose, in one man's opinion, is to get you to agree in writing that a serious downdraft in your account is something you not only understand, but accept.

As you may remember, most questionnaires give you the option of choosing between varieties of portfolios varying from aggressive to conservative in their range of return possibilities. Generally, they look something like this: Portfolio A has an average annual return of 7.39% and has a historic range of returns that 95% of the time falls between 9.2% and negative 8.3%.

Or, behind curtain number two where Carol Merrill (if you're under 40, Google her) is now standing, you could pick the one that earned an average 9.1% historically with a range 95% of the time between 11.5% and negative 13.2%. (These are just examples, people...not real... fake... kidding, etc. Please put the phone down, Mr. Lawyer.)

Many, if not most, of you will almost always be sold to the middle on these types of things. You will pick something between the most aggressive and the most conservative for the same reason most of you will order a medium soft drink when presented with three options. (Jim Morrison was right, "people are strange.") Now, after you have gone through this exercise and agreed that you are okay with the volatility you just initialed next to, most advisors set about giving it to you. In short and once again, "BE CAREFUL WHAT YOU ASK FOR."

First of all, most of these returns are run within the context of the "95% of the time this happens" rule. Using this logic, I guess we should assume that for the next 90 years or so nothing bad is coming our way, since 2000-2001 and 2007-2008 were well outside the numbers represented by most of these estimates.

The risk you take should be nothing more than a byproduct of the risk you "must" take. If you are 60 years old and have saved diligently and thoughtfully over the last 40 years, odds are you do NOT need to take much, if any, risk. If you walk into my office with a million bucks and explain to me that you only require this nest egg to produce $20,000.00 per year in income, simple math tells me that you need to earn 2% per year to be successful (ignoring inflation for a minute). Why in the world would you "try" to earn 10%?

Conversely, if you bring in that same million big ones into my office and intimate to me that you need it to produce $100,000.00 per year, then more than likely, I am going to suggest you buy lottery tickets because "conservative" is a non-starter for you and your 10% withdrawal rate. In the end, the risk you take is a direct byproduct of the responsibility you have shouldered in the past and will shoulder in the future. Risk, as the term implies, is fraught with peril, and while occasionally it is proportionately rewarded, more times than not, it isn't.

Your goal should be to control your need for risk by saving and spending in a manner that allows for it.

Recently, one of the younger partners in our office came to me about a discussion he was having with a client. The client was pushing back a bit because the account he had opened, for the year, was in the red a little bit and he, like most people, took issue with it. The client's discussion centered on the idea that he wanted to be conservative, and if the account did not come up to the breakeven point by year's-end he would likely do something different.

From the young advisor's perspective, he wanted me to help him articulate the benefits of long-term investing, risk management, and the numerous other services we pride ourselves on over here at our Rugby Street "International Headquarters."

The more I quizzed the young advisor, the more I realized that the issue was not one of misunderstanding on the client's part; it was in fact a misunderstanding on the advisor's part. Like all well-intended professionals, our hero was sure that our solution was "everyone's" solution. I, in fact, think the opposite. I believe what we do is for a select group of folks who have very specific needs and problems to which we might provide solutions.

Some people, like this client after further review, were likely not a good fit for us. This client had saved a decent, although not huge, amount of money and coupled that with a frugal lifestyle which allowed him to survive, and in his own way thrive, on absolutely ZERO return. In short, why would he need us?

We are in the risk-management/goal attainment business, which is largely predicated on the need many (not all) people have to earn a better than ZERO return with controlled risk in order to meet their lifestyle objectives. So, if a guy needs to earn zero, he does not need us.

We could argue the value in service, forms administration, distributions, taxes and the like, but not today. We live in a nation of people who largely spend their time trying to get risk-type returns in risk-free investments. What I mean by that is people love risk—as long as it is UP! It's the down they don't like so much.

People like to think that somewhere out there they are going to meet someone who can get them 10% with no risk. When one guy tells them they can earn 7% or 8% per year and they will experience some turbulence and likely a down year or two over a decade, they scoff and say *no thanks*. Conversely, when a guy you know tells you about a guy he knows who can get you 12% with no risk, you should be thinking, "Well now, Mr. Madoff, come right in and have a seat!"

It is this same mentality that causes you to buy things that have already gone up in value. "Mr. and Mrs. Brown, can I interest you in this investment that earned negative 20% last year?" "WHAT!?

Of course, you cannot because that is clearly risky." "My bad, Mr. and Mrs. Brown, let's look at this one that was up 20% last year." "Now that's what I'm talking about!" (high fives his wife)

You believe that your new friend has shown you the investment with the least risk *because it has already gone up?*

Yes, that's what you do—admit it. It will happen five times in the hour I am typing this.

An advisor/broker/insurance agent/whatever will likely take the easy way out by appealing to your pattern-seeking/risk-avoiding inner voice, and you, my friends, will fall for it every time. You will only climb out on the ledge when the elevator is on the 10th floor, but not when it's on the first?

As I often do, I will cite the great Warren Buffett who is "fearful when others are greedy and greedy when others are fearful." Warren Buffett would rather have his eyes poked out than buy anything that is not beaten down a bit. My friends, risk is not your enemy; a lack of understanding it is.

Consider the Counterfactuals

This past week, I watched a documentary on Robert McNamara, whom some of you will remember as the former Secretary of Defense under Presidents Kennedy and, ultimately, Johnson. McNamara had the dubious honor of serving during the Vietnam War and was instrumental in all that occurred, good, bad, or indifferent.

What struck me about this man was first his intellect and then his understanding of what happened and, for the purposes of our discussion, what might have happened. Now, I am not bold enough to have a strong opinion on the value of his service during this difficult period (especially since I was nine when the war ended), but I do think one point made in this film is transferable to the business of investing.

He made the point in this interview that people will always judge his effectiveness, and really any leader's effectiveness, on the actual outcomes associated with the event. Makes sense, right? What did you do, and what was the outcome? His point was that while the outcome may not have been great by most standards, what *could it have been* if he were not calling the shots? Would it have been worse or would it have been better? This, my friends, is the counterfactual. We know what *did* happen—but we don't know what could have happened, or at least we don't bother to think about what could have happened.

History lesson aside, how does this tie into investing? Recently, I met with a client of mine who was, it is fair to say, a little frustrated that the account had not gone up as much as the overall stock market these past few months. (Of course, I remind you this is also a person who, a few months ago, was convinced the world was going to end and all but insisted I put all of their money in gold, corn seed, and gunpowder.)

Most of us consider only what did happen as opposed to what *could* have happened when we look at our investments—we forget the counterfactual. You cannot build a portfolio that makes the distraught and bunker-building person you were back in December content AND that will also participate 100% in the market we've had over the last few months. It won't work.

Our job as investment professionals is to consider what *could* happen. We need to know what the possible outcomes for a portfolio are when we build it, and so should you. If you want to eliminate the possibility of a double-digit decline in any given year, you have to accept that you will not be the benefactor of 100% of all the quick bursts the market is prone to—and that is okay.

If you have a portfolio today that participated 100% in this market upturn you are probably pretty happy with what DID happen. It is also important at this point for you to ask: What could happen?

Bitcoin

Bitcoin could go to $100k for all I know. Bitcoin is no different than tech stocks were several years ago, or gold mines were in the 1800s. The people who are going to get rich are the ones who will sell it to you now. The Winklevoss twins who bought it at $500 are saying it's going to $100k. It's not impossible that Bitcoin will be the greatest thing ever. In the meantime, a few people will get rich and a lot of people will get their teeth kicked in, because they're all going to be late to the game.

It's amazing to me that people will see something that's $100, like Bitcoin was a few years ago, and say, "There's a lot of risk in that. I don't know what it is, I don't know how it works." Then, when it's $60,000, they *still* don't know what it is or how it works, but suddenly it appears to have no risk in it.

I could be missing the boat. The beauty is, I don't care. To be a successful investor, you must take a "good for you" attitude to missed opportunities. The list of great investments I missed out on is immense. Again, I don't care. Good for you if you bought Apple in 1990 or Microsoft in 1980. Good for you if you bought Bitcoin at $10, and good for you if you bought the winning Powerball ticket. (Well maybe, a high percentage of lottery winners end up bankrupt and pissed off.)

In short, don't be distracted by what you did not do or what someone else *did*. Build your process and remain committed to it.

Here's How to Handle Risk: Do Math the Way Institutional Endowments Do Math

People, on average, are driven by two things: fear and greed. Fear is that feeling you get when you look at your brokerage or 401(k) statement and realize you are not saving enough to provide the retirement of your dreams. Greed is when you look at your neighbor's new Mercedes and realize he is clearly doing something illegal and is not nearly as good looking as you are.

The net result in both cases is the need to get higher returns in order to fix the aforementioned issues. Higher returns? What does that mean? Generally, it means you want your return to be higher than whatever it currently is, and if possible higher than what your neighbor is pretending to be getting. This need to outperform some mythical benchmark is generally the downfall of most investors.

"But Scott," you say, like you always do at this point in our show, "don't I *want* to 'outperform?'"

Sure, you do, but outperform *what?*

There are numerous benchmarks you could try to outperform. Go ahead, pick one. Shall we outperform the Dow this week, or how 'bout the S&P 500? I know, let's outperform the commodity index and next week we'll vow to beat the Shanghai Index.

Much like in my sporting life, there is always something or someone better. One year it's bonds (okay, for 20 years it's been bonds), and some years it's Pork Bellies. (God, I love bacon!)

The pros who run endowments do not feel the need to chase indexes or returns for that matter. They never get caught (almost never) in the washing machine of what did well yesterday, because they don't care. Large endowments for colleges and/or pensions have a process they follow and the only benchmark they care about is success and achieving it.

The boards of these types of institutions have their own benchmarks that go something like this: We at the S. Brown University (accepting mascot ideas now) have $1 million dollars. We expect to take in $100,000.00 in donations over the next year. Looking into the next year, SBU expects to fund two scholarships at $50k each and build a band shell which will cost us another $50k. Quick math tells us that $1 million plus $100k in donations minus $150,000.00 in expenses equals a $50,000.00 deficit, or 5% in needed return for our objectives to be met.

Now, the next part is critical. It is incumbent on our board at SBU to keep from sacrificing the principal our donors have given us; thus, we must *only take enough risk* to meet our objective. Taking more risk is not only a bad idea with unknown results, it is a fiduciary failure.

The need to achieve success is not only the way institutions manage money, but it is why they generally outperform you. If you took the same methodology and applied it to your finances, I believe you too would be more likely to find success—because *that* is your goal, not a return. What do you have in total assets, what do you expect to save in the years leading up to retirement, and how much do you anticipate spending?

Do the math, and at the end, like our favorite college SBU, you will find your needed rate of return and the true determinant of your return goal. The only benchmark that matters is the one that includes your personal version of success. 500 random stocks have nothing to do with it.

The Bottom Line on Risk

People want risk returns without taking the risk, and that can't be done. It's the existence of that risk that gives you the return. Absent the risk, your return sucks. That's the choice you make. Do I want the risk? How can I be thoughtful about the risk? How can I mitigate the risk? Generally, time mitigates risk. If you buy AT&T today at $35 and it goes to $32, so what? If you hold it for the next 10 years, it'll probably be $60. It might be $25 first, but time in equity markets pretty much mitigates risk.

Key Chapter 11 Takeaways:

- You have less risk tolerance than you think you do.
- The risk you take should be nothing more than a byproduct of the risk you "must" take.
- There's no such thing as high returns with no risk.
- Consider not only what *did* happen, consider what *could've* happened.
- Buying things that already went up in value is not a risk-proof strategy.
- Do math the way institutional endowments do math.

Section Three

For My Advisor Friends

Chapter 12
Think Long-Term

It's not about any single accomplishment. It is about the cycle of endless refinement and continuous improvement. Ultimately, it is your commitment to the process that will determine your progress. ~James Clear

Just as a client needs to think long-term when choosing a financial advisor, so too do my colleagues. We are also in a long-term relationship when we take on a new client. Therefore, advisors need to recognize, once and for all, that these quick sales are not the answer. Selling products that you don't really understand or know much about, just because they look good or sound good, or because you just went to a steak dinner, is not the way toward building a book of business.

The person with a nice suit who just said, "Hey, you should sell our product?" Listening to them is fast a path to nowhere. That's the short term.

Be willing to provide value on an ongoing basis without always getting paid for it. Be ready to have a conversation about a 529 plan. It's a pain in the butt and you're never going to get paid for it. But it's something your client needs. So, be ready to help.

When your entrepreneurial client (PS: I just had this conversation) calls you and says, "Hey, man, I got a chance to put a million bucks in this marketing company that's going to make me pretty good money," be ready to have that conversation. Know that million dollars is leaving, so it's going to cost you some money because you manage it. But be willing to help him do that if it's a good idea.

Because later, when he makes $10 million off the million, it's going to come back to you.

Again, don't be transactional. Don't say, "Well, you should borrow the money," or, "This is a terrible investment." No. Be there to help them even if it hurts you in the short term – because in the long run, they'll recognize that you didn't try and talk them out of something just because it hurt you. You didn't talk them out of it for selfish reasons. You need to be a partner to these people and you need to understand the products that you're selling as well as the costs associated with them.

Next, you need to provide a higher level of service than most people are providing. Most people are selling products and then they're looking for another person to sell products. I don't think they're bad people. I don't think they're trying to rip anybody off. However, I do think these short-term product sellers are not putting their best foot forward. I do think they're failing to provide value over and above the guy or gal in the cubby next door. Right? Because they're all doing the same thing.

I've been doing this for 36 years and I am arguably successful, any way you want to measure it. And I'm telling you, the day I decided to stop being transactional was the day I really started to grow something meaningful. The day I decided, "I'm not doing this anymore. I'm not selling products because some guy in a suit driving a Mercedes told me to," was the day I started to win. I said, "I am going to get very serious about my craft. I am going to understand – as best anybody can – markets. I'm going to understand tax implications. I'm going to understand everything I can possibly understand about this business, and I'm not going to push it on anybody."

I *like* to understand long-term planning.

The irony is once you're in this for a decade or two, and you'll become good at it, people will find you. People will sense it. They will smell it. The reverse is also true. Investors, clients, and potential clients can smell desperation. They can smell that you have a Porsche in the parking lot you need to make the payment on, which is why they need to buy the latest thing. They can smell it and this approach is, frankly, a terrible sales tool. Desperation is easy to spot.

Once you legitimately don't care anything about anything other than providing value to the client, that is when you will be very well compensated.

Don't Pretend

Don't pretend to know something that you don't know. You can't predict the market.

Don't pretend you're something you're not.

You don't know what Microsoft's going to do tomorrow. You don't know what Apple is going to do. I could make a list of 100 advisors who told me about some ridiculous stock they were sure was going to do gangbusters and ended up doing nothing. You don't know, any more than the client does, what the market is going to do day to day, month to month, sometimes even year to year. What you do know is that historically, with good planning, thoughtful security selection, and intentional risk management, you can get a client to material success.

You can help them with emotions, sure, but you can also get them to material success. However, if you pretend when they walk in that you know things you don't know, you're in trouble. If you say,

"Oh yeah, I think you should be all in because the market is going to do great this year," and that doesn't happen? You're done with that client. You have promised them something you can't deliver.

If you say to them, "I have no idea what the market is going to do this year. Here are the economic indicators. Here's what I see with inflation. Here's what I see with unemployment. Here's what I see with interest rates."

You can have those conversations and these talks are somewhat meaningful, but at the end of the day, you could know interest rates and you can know where inflation is projected to go and you could know what unemployment is going to be and *still be wrong about the market*. The brightest minds in the industry are wrong very frequently. So, rather than commit yourself to something you can't deliver, which is forecasting or crystal ball-type stuff, focus on the planning, focus on the security selection, focus on the cost control, focus on the tax implications. Focus on the outcomes.

If you give me a million dollars and you need $80,000 a year in income and you get $20,000 from Social Security, I need to get you 6%. So, I might say, "Historically, you can get 6% by doing this, this, and this, and that would be the most conservative way forward. Statistically, there's a 90% chance this will work out. And, if we get down the road and it's looking like it's a little wonky, we will make some adjustments."

Really, this is about the process. It is not about crystal balls. It is not about markets. The market could go flat for the next five years for all I know. What I do know is if we do the right planning, it won't affect us as much.

Kay Chapter 12 Takeaways:

- Think long term.
- Don't pretend to know something you cannot know.
- Put the client's needs ahead of your own.
- Develop a process and stick to it.

I've Never Made Anyone Rich

Conclusion
Same As It Ever Was

You may ask yourself; how did I get here?
~David Byrne

Much like the 1980s song "Once in a Lifetime" suggests, you probably spend a fair amount of time each day trying to predict what's to come. Indeed, *how did we get here* and *what will happen tomorrow* are often the domain of those who mistakenly think there is order to this thing we call life, and more importantly for our purposes, "investing."

Many of you spend an inordinate amount of time trying to predict the unpredictable. You use all kinds of Ouija board tactics and misguided biases to try to make sense of the randomness that is human existence. Oftentimes, a client (or would-be client) will explain to me this is all so very predictable if we just look for the right indicators. If a portfolio manager has a good year, and subsequently the short-sighted media gives that person undue attention in an effort to boost ratings and sell more stuff, many will flock to hear and or invest with said person.

Each year, Morningstar, the ubiquitous rater of all things *investment*, gives mutual funds a star rating. These ratings range from one to five stars, with five being – in their not-so-humble opinion – the best of the best. To quote our friends the Talking Heads, *you may tell yourself:*

"This is how I will pick my mutual funds going forward. I will simply wait for Morningstar to rate funds and pick only the five stars and then I too...will have a Large Automobile and a Beautiful Wife." (It's in the song, don't get too worked up.)

The problem with this strategy is it employs two biases that, in my opinion (which is not humble at all), are an investor's worst enemy: *hindsight bias* and *immediacy bias*.

Hindsight bias is the belief that you more or less knew (once it actually happened) that a given outcome was likely despite zero evidence to support this thesis. An example of this would be the guy crowing at a party (easy on the free drinks, Sport) that he saw the "whole thing" coming. Whole thing? Yes, the whole thing. He saw the financial crisis of '08 despite there being no evidence he got out of real estate or went to cash just before all hell broke loose.

He saw the market rebounding hard and fast from the March Covid lows despite the fact that he stayed in cash the entire rest of the year. You see, the problem with using past events and, more correctly, recent events to gauge future events, is that your instincts are more often than not wrong. Sometimes they're a little wrong and more frequently, they're very wrong.

Our friends at Morningstar provide a very important service. They tell us what "did" happen, which is useful. How did a fund or investment react to high interest rates, a recession, or geopolitical strife and the like? The problem is that statistically, a five-star mutual fund is more likely to become a one-star mutual fund than remain a five-star fund. In short, we are seeking patterns where none exist. Hindsight bias, then, is the belief you knew something you very likely did not.

Recency bias is the belief that whatever happened yesterday is likely to persist. (See Florida weather as a lesson in humility.) Recency bias is looking at your statement, finding the three stocks that are down, deciding to sell them, and adding to the three that are the best performers – giving zero respect to the cycles that have existed in securities and economies for centuries. Today's stinker is more likely to shine in the period ahead than today's rock star.

If we know anything, it's that things change. History may not repeat itself, but as Mark Twain famously said, "it often rhymes." The rhyme is the randomness. What doesn't change is your inability to predict the ebbs and flows of these cycles in advance of them.

We invest because we believe in the fundamental soundness of our capitalistic system, not because we know how the system will react to any given stimulus or what the next stimulus will be. To that end, I have correctly predicted that our risk markets would bring long-term growth, generally better than those in "fixed" and "riskless" investments over my now 37-year career. The things I have failed to predict are both numerous and notorious: Covid, 9/11, the housing crisis, Russia invading Ukraine, Bernie Madoff, most presidential elections, the impact of social media, Elon Musk, Google, Amazon, and, of course, the world domination of Taylor Swift.

Folks at our humble little firm now manage over $2 billion in total assets, so we do our best to anticipate long-term cyclical shifts. We understand the math of bond durations and the correlation of loose Fed policy and corporate liquidity. We understand bad things will happen, but know our best defense is sound principles and a disciplined long-term outlook. "Red stocks" will likely not remain that way forever and "green stocks" (the up ones you like so much) will eventually spend some time out of favor. Knowing that we don't know exactly when is way more important than incorrectly thinking the opposite.

In the end, thoughtful planning and discipline will determine whether you live in a "beautiful house or a shotgun shack," not seeing false patterns and giving in to untrustworthy biases.

"Let the days go by, the water will still be flowing underground."

It Was Never About the Money

Most financially successful people are really not enamored with money. They get what it is and they understand its value and its usefulness, but it is not the end all, be all for them. At their core, most financially successful people do not allow money to control them and never have.

It's not that they don't like to have it or they don't dig the new car it may buy them from time to time, but most of my top clients have money because it's a byproduct of how they live and who they are, not the object of their desire. Some people fret over every purchase and every cost, spending countless hours trying to find the cheapest *this* or the best deal on *that*.

Those with a scarcity mentality are often worried about who is out to get them. They believe the only good transaction is one where they get their half of the deal and a good portion of the other person's half. Many simply focus too much on the transaction rather than on the big picture.

Investing is hopefully something you'll do for a while. In fact, most people will do it for a lifetime when they do it well. So, what seems like an important transaction today, in the big scheme of things when you look back, won't be what matters. What matters is if you're successful. We make a transaction quickly because we believe it'll feel good if we make the trade and it does well. But we're apprehensive emotionally because if it doesn't do well, we're going to feel bad.

You can remove all that fear by being a long-term investor. By not doing transactions, but instead making investments that you believe will work in the long term. Some of them will, some won't. In four or five years, there'll be obvious reasons some were a mistake. But most of them, if they're thoughtful investments and you let them play out, will be fine. If you've created a relationship with your financial advisor or educated yourself to the point where you don't need to create a relationship with a financial advisor, you're good. Of course, the latter also requires you to enjoy managing your assets and giving up your time to do it.

If you choose to develop a relationship with somebody that you hope will be your advisor for the next 20, 30, or even 50 years, it should be someone you can grow with and bounce things off. It's someone who will do the administrative work and who will keep you from making poor emotional decisions, who will do the research when you're buying longer-term investments, someone who will talk to you about tax implications.

To me, the whole point is getting away from the transactions, which is what Wall Street companies want you to focus on because they don't care whether you win, lose, or draw; they don't care if you buy or sell. They just care that you do *something*. Because if you do something, that makes them money. Building relationships matters more. Get away from the idea that you can trade successfully. You cannot. It's been proven time and time and time again: people who trade more regularly than the average person are less likely to be successful in the long run.

Most of my top clients don't even call much, and I have to tackle them by the ankles to get them to come in and review their accounts. They are busy growing their businesses and building relationships that, ironically, can lead to more money.

That's right: the less they are controlled by money, the more they seem to have. Please don't misunderstand. If I load up and head to the Caymans they will, of course, care and likely form a posse, but short of that, they mostly tend to focus on their passions, both personal and professional.

Recently, this point was driven home for me as I visited a client of mine who was dying of cancer, Jim (not his real name) was a giant of a man, both physically and spiritually. He and his wife of over 30 years were lifelong school teachers who, I am sure, never made what many would consider a ton of money. They lived simple yet fulfilling lives, never driving fancy cars or moving from their modest home in South Florida. On average, I would visit them two to three times per year and we would discuss life and their mission, which was teaching and children.

Jim was passionate about kids, and especially about teaching them music. He and I would talk guitar and my dream of maybe someday retiring to teach as well. At the end of each conversation, I would kind of force him around to discussing his and his wife's money, which he would somewhat reluctantly do. Usually, he could tolerate a few minutes and then back to Neil Young or Eric Clapton we would go.

I tell you this because Jim and his wife had accumulated well over seven figures in assets simply by focusing on life and their dedication to children. The difficult part for me, driving home from that recent visit, was realizing he had worked his whole life to accumulate that money, and now literally a month after retiring, would never get to enjoy the money they had worked so hard to accumulate. Yet as I drove north on the Turnpike that day, it hit me all at once: it was never about the money. The money was there because he was simply too busy living his passion and doing for others.

11 Books Everyone Should Read

- *The Millionaire Next Door* by Thomas J. Stanley
- *Rich Dad Poor Dad* by Robert Kyosaki
- *Conspiracy of the Rich* by Robert Kyosaki
- *The Psychology of Money* by Morgan Housel
- *Think and Grow Rich* by Napoleon Hill
- *Win Friends and Influence People* by Dale Carnegie
- *The Tao of Charlie Munger* by David Clark
- *38 Letters from J.D. Rockefeller to his son* by G. Ng
- *Tools of Titans* by Tim Ferris
- *Fooled by Randomness* by Nassim Taleb
- *Your Money and Your Brain* by Jason Zwieg

I've Never Made Anyone Rich

Reflection

Working on this book was a pleasure, and the reason is simple: it's full of good news. Sure, money and all the baggage that goes along with that one word tends to stress people out (understatement), but the main point of these preceding 200 pages is that it doesn't have to.

Comfort, security, and even wealth is well within reach for most people as long as they avoid a few all-too-common pitfalls. You won't become wealthy or secure constantly buying things you can't really afford, spending your time trying to find the year's hottest stock, chasing yesterday's returns, or pouring your hard-earned money into the lottery. You just won't. You also won't find riches haggling for a deal or undervaluing the professionals helping you get where you're trying to go.

What Scott has done in this book is taken what can be a complex and fraught topic—money and investing—and distilled it all down to a few simple principles that anyone can follow. As I see it, these principles are to earn at least a little more than you spend each year, work with an honest financial advisor who will listen to you and build a process, pay him or her what they're worth, and then relax and focus on other things in your life. Focus on what you're good at and what brings you happiness, whether that's doctoring, teaching, parenting, writing, building, or starting a business. Establish a saving habit, honor your investing habit, and turn off the cable news.

Once you find this simple rhythm and learn to let go, the money will flow.

There's no reason to choke the life out of the process by chasing investing trends, worrying about the stock of the day, finding out how high the Powerball jackpot has grown, or logging in to learn who is tweeting what. That's all noise designed to make you crazy.

Breathe.

The good news is clear: once you get your money ducks in a row, you'll be free to become the calm, generous, and grounded individual you know you are—person who can stop worrying and start living.

~Laura Schaefer

Acknowledgments

I'd like to thank every advisor I've ever worked with. I've learned from each and every one of you. The list of great advisors is super long, but special thanks to Paul Wood and the Squid (Syd Gomez). What a long strange trip it's been. In addition, I'd like to thank every client who has entrusted me and my team with what is often the result of an entire life's labor in the form of money. That has never been and will never be lost on me.

Thanks to my two amazing and super talented kids (I know everybody says that...I swear it's true). Lastly, to the two amazing women in my life, Martha and Linda: I could never have come this far without the two of you protecting me from my own intensity.

www.ingramcontent.com/pod-product-compliance
Lightning Source LLC
Chambersburg PA
CBHW020636220526
45464CB00001B/172